A Radical Rethinking of Sexuality and Schooling

Curriculum, Cultures, and (Homo)Sexualities
Edited by James T. Sears

A Radical Rethinking of Sexuality and Schooling

Status Quo or Status Queer?

Eric Rofes

ROWMAN & LITTLEFIELD PUBLISHERS, INC.
Lanham • Boulder • New York • Toronto • Oxford

ROWMAN & LITTLEFIELD PUBLISHERS, INC.

Published in the United States of America
by Rowman & Littlefield Publishers, Inc.
A wholly owned subsidiary of The Rowman & Littlefield Publishing Group, Inc.
4501 Forbes Boulevard, Suite 200, Lanham, MD 20706
www.rowmanlittlefield.com

P.O. Box 317, Oxford OX2 9RU, UK

British Library Cataloguing in Publication Information Available

Library of Congress Cataloging-in-Publication Data

Rofes, Eric E., 1954–
  A radical rethinking of sexuality and schooling: Status quo or status queer? / Eric Rofes.
      p. cm. — (Curriculum, cultures, and (homo)sexualities)
  Includes bibliographical references and index.
  ISBN 0-7425-4194-0 (cloth : alk. paper) — ISBN 0-7425-4195-9 (pbk. alk. paper)
  1. Homosexuality and education—United States. 2. Gay students—United States. 3.
Gay teachers—United States. I. Title II. Series.

LC192.6.R64 2005
371.826'64—dc22

                                                              2004022276

Printed in the United States of America

⊗™ The paper used in this publication meets the minimum requirements of American
National Standard for Information Sciences—Permanence of Paper for Printed Library
Materials, ANSI/NISO Z39.48-1992.

This book is dedicated to a special group of politically active friends and organizing comrades who, for over twenty-five years, have encouraged me at every opportunity to move from status quo to status queer:

Richard Burns, Kate Clinton, Amy Hoffman, Will Seng, Roberta Stone, and Urvashi Vaid

Contents

Acknowledgments

I would like to thank colleagues who assisted me during the writing of this book. Because it pulls together my work in disparate fields—education, queer studies, activism, HIV prevention, and teacher preparation—I have drawn support from many sources. Students who have enrolled in my course on gay and lesbian issues in schools, both at University of California–Berkeley and, now, at Humboldt State University, have offered countless perspectives into the issues tackled in this text.

I have been grateful to Maria Corral-Ribordy, Sue Burcell, David Orphal, and Ryan Darling for particular insights and to Professor John Hurst of Berkeley for encouraging me to initiate this course when I was a graduate student in 1995. Other Humboldt State University faculty and staff members— Christina Accomando, Ann Diver-Stamnes, Patty Yancey, Kim Berry, Keri Gelenian, Sheila Rocker-Heppe, Diane Ryerson, Eric Van Duzer, Cathleen Rafferty, and Denice Helwig—have supported this work by providing me with colleagues on campus with whom I could discuss challenges in the research and writing process and my own shifting thinking about work on sexuality and schooling.

Likewise, I am grateful to members of the San Francisco Study Group on Sex and Politics for inspiring my thinking about sex, gender, and social change over the past ten years, especially Martha Baer, Pat Egan, David Steinberg, Jason Daniels, Julie Leavitt, Will Carr, Kathy Sisson, Will Seng, Sara Miles, Francisco Gonzalez, Gayle Rubin, Tim Vollmer, Dara Sklar, and Liz Highleyman. Colleagues who have worked with me at numerous health summits or HIV prevention meetings and shifted my thinking on gay men and education in valuable ways include Chris Bartlett, Richard Elovich, Daniel Wolfe, Gary Dowsett, Marj Plumb, Michael Ross, Will Nutland, Scott

Pegues, Gordon Youngman, Linda Pippin, Carlos Velazquez, Peter Keough, Kane Race, Ralph Bolton, David Nimmons, and Brent Allen. As I was completing this manuscript, I was working with Susan Talburt and Mary Lou Rasmussen on a separate collection titled *Youth and Sexualities: Pleasure, Subversion, and Insubordination in and out of Schools* (2004), and our lively exchanges helped clarify key issues in my thinking about queers, sexuality, gender, and schooling.

Most of these chapters have been developed out of papers I have presented at professional conferences and annual meetings of various professional groups. I am grateful to colleagues within these organizations—the American Sociological Association, Pacific Sociological Association, American Education Research Association, California Council of Teacher Educators, American Anthropological Association, and the American Public Health Association—who have provided me with feedback, challenges, and quirky insights.

Tom Hehir, Janet Ferone, Jeff Brandenberg, Daniel Derdula, Fran Reich, Diane Sabin, John Sharkey, Dennis Nix, Bob Brown, Margo Okazawa-Rey, Gwyn Kirk, and Nicholas Govindan have shared much of this journey with me and supported my writing efforts. Crispin Hollings continued to provide encouragement and insights throughout the process.

Unanticipated encouragement came to me at a critical moment at an annual meeting of the American Education Research Association from Jonathan Silin, Bill Ayers, Celia Oyler, and Pat Griffin. I am grateful to Jim Sears for his enthusiastic response to the manuscript and for welcoming the book into his series at Rowman & Littlefield. Christine Miller, a graduate student at Humboldt State University in our environment and community program, worked diligently as my assistant during the 2002–2003 term and served as an editor and text reviewer of this entire manuscript.

I am especially grateful to Urvashi Vaid, who introduced me to the book's title through her powerful speeches, astute political writings, and several decades as a comrade and friend.

1

Beyond the Bruising Sites of Boyhood

This book is about me. It is about a third-grade boy forced to play sports when he'd rather be inside playing with his sister's necklaces and rings. It is about the seventh-grade student, seen as gentle and girlish, harassed in junior high hallways and chased home from school. It is about the high school over-achiever, not only compensating for gender violations with elevated test scores and energetic service to the school, but also diligently working to earn himself the relative safety provided by high-track classes and school leader-ship positions.

Yet it is also about the little boy who against formidable odds chose coop-erative play over competition, sharing over selfishness, gentleness over toughness. Is it possible that my desire to play with the girls, while often in-terpreted so simplistically to mean I wanted to *be* a girl and not a boy, actu-ally indicated my attraction to the values and rituals more common to girl cul-ture than to boy culture?

While many understand gender-nonconforming youth as simply their be-ing "born that way," is it possible that children enact a type of agency that doesn't comfortably fit within the traditional ways we understand cognitive choice and mindful decision making? I believe my moral development and the values I embraced may have been tightly linked to my refusal to conform to the proper image and behavior assigned to boys. The messages that came my way from all sides—from my father, peers, siblings, school teachers, neighbors—clearly demanded that I adhere to the socially appropriate behav-ior for boys. I hemmed and hawed; I prevaricated; I resisted.

Ultimately, I opted otherwise.

The literature on student resistance and on social production and reproduc-tion has traditionally focused on students' rebelling against the rules and regulations of our education system with the values and politics embodied in that system. Studies of school dropouts, students with "behavior problems," and those with lackadaisical attitudes toward academic achievement examine ways in which complex social and cultural forces drive students to resist the socialization and disciplinary work of schools and ultimately end up reproducing the status quo (Fine 1991; Stevenson and Ellis 1993; Willis 1977). The students typically studied by resistance researchers are the "bad" boys and the "bad" girls—the hoods, gang members, troublemakers, sluts, and smart alecs (Eckert 1989; Willis 1977).

Yet, I believe an argument can be made for understanding gender-nonconforming children and adolescents as resisters—resisters to the patriarchal gender inculcation that occurs within most schools, family units, and youth peer groups. My boyish effeminate hand gestures can alternately be understood as either genetic errors that required social approbation to correct or rebellious acts committed to undermining the macho values constantly thrust on me. My determination to skip rope, enjoy hopscotch, and play with dolls rather than join the boys in kickball or dodge ball might suggest an ambitious intent to create an alternative social world for myself outside the bruising sites of boyhood.

DOMINATION, SUBMISSION, AND CONTEMPORARY CONSTRUCTIONS OF CHILDHOOD

This book is about gay issues in education, and it attempts to conceptualize lesbian, gay, bisexual, and transgender (LGBT) youth and gender-nonconforming youth as something beyond passive victims of sexist and homophobic assaults. While not denying the powerful and sometimes unrelenting violence visited on the bodies and souls of these youth, this book aims to broaden our perspectives and shift our analytical position on this population. We can see queer youth and other outsiders as vulnerable or fragile, but we can also see them as daring, powerful, and rebellious. We can understand them as resilient survivors of repeated traumas, or we can see LGBT youth as engaged in a lengthy effort to undermine constrictive gender roles and create alternative childhoods and adolescences. Or, we can see both.

My own experience suggests that gender-deviant children may not proceed through their everyday lives in a constant state of suffering, terror, or sadness; it suggests that we might regard these alternative spaces and sites that these children create for themselves as places of hope, celebration, and respite. This book is about a boy who created his own sites of safety and happiness, his face buried in *Wizard of Oz* books or his eyes and ears enraptured by after-school soap operas. It is about the Cub Scout who sought joy in nature; the boy who found daily inspiration in showtunes; the nine-year-old fascinated by his Avon-lady mother's monthly cache of green-tinted bottles, shiny silver tubes, and containers of exotic-smelling bubble-bath oils. It is about the young teen who, on some level, sized up his life chances and strategically plotted a path that would bring him a modicum of safety, success, and personal satisfaction while maintaining his integrity and dissident values.

Americans often create narratives of childhood that do a tremendous disservice to the complex day-to-day reality of our early years. Traditional accounts of childhood innocence still maintain tremendous salience, as individuals choose to recall warm family holidays, toboggan rides down snowy hills, and hot summer days at local swimming holes. We embrace comforting tropes of loving parents, safe neighborhoods, and community prosperity. We then live our adult lives as castaways from the Eden of childhood, determined to compensate for our own fall from grace by re-creating these idylls for the children of today. We bookend our lives by telling ourselves that retirement and old age will be a return to the supposed ease and innocence of our childhoods, and we imagine old people as children, somehow freed from the contradictions, complexities, and challenges of life.

Over the past thirty years, our culture has paired this original story with an equally powerful narrative of childhood trauma. Perhaps spurred as much by twelve-step programs and the public exposure of long-suppressed violations—such as child abuse and neglect, incest, schoolyard bullying, and sexual violence and harassment—we remember our childhoods solely as sites of peril, terror, and deep, sustained sadness. We come together around new tropes of dysfunctional families, absent fathers, vindictive mothers, and the terrible loneliness we felt in our victimization and social isolation. We become determined to protect today's children from similar fates, and we marshal our resources and personal energies toward child saving. We become accustomed to searching for the sources of our current unhappiness and adult failings in the persecution we experienced as children. We imagine ourselves as martyrs to those early years, fated to live out unfulfilled lives because of the damage wreaked on us in childhood.

I once organized my own life story from this vantage point. I made sense of everything—from my relationship failures to my intense commitment to my work to my inability to control my anger—by linking them to my family of origin. In addition to blaming Mom or Dad (sometimes both) as the source of my current unhappiness, I could also blame my childhood experience as a gentle boy mocked and derided by bullies. My reasoning at the time was that, because others victimized me, I avoid conflict with others; I assume the role of peacemaker; and I shut down when the yelling occurs.

If we've learned anything from the first two decades of research into the sociology of childhood, it is that this stage of life is complex, driven by powerful and competing forces, and rarely reduced to simple description or painted in broad brushstrokes (Austin and Willard 1998a; Brake 1980; Skolnick 1976). In the late 1970s, early in my career as a schoolteacher, I was struck by the gap between the ways in which adults see children and the ways in which children see themselves. As the economy shifted and the women's movement gained speed, my middle school students in a liberal Cambridge, Massachusetts, school were among the first cohorts of children to collectively have foisted on them the process of divorce. I recall recognizing that seventeen of my twenty students had endured family breakup; I then used this realization to explain a range of classroom tensions and individual student failings. I developed a huge empathy for these "poor children" and felt their suffering deeply, even though I had not experienced divorce in my family. At the same time, divorce became an easy excuse for a student's failing an exam, forgetting to do homework, or acting sullen or aggressive in school.

Only when I began exploring the experience of divorce with the students did I learn that many of my students had not experienced their parents' divorces in the way I had imagined. Many had found aspects of the divorce that provided new benefits and relieved longstanding tensions. One girl told me about her delight in having two different homes with two different sets of rules. She felt able to marry her personal tastes and daily moods to the proper home environment. A boy discussed his relief of finally living in homes without a lot of arguments or drama. He believed life after divorce offered an opportunity to focus on himself rather than on comforting his parents or serving as a mediator between two adults on a regular basis. Whereas few students would ever wish divorce on their families, these children, ranging from ten to fourteen years old, were not only able to note the benefits and liabilities of their transformed situation but could also understand the nuanced ways in which they were personally affected by their changing family structures (Rofes 1981). I learned something valuable from those students.

My own childhood cannot be simplistically characterized as either good or bad. This would be like reducing one's entire life to a one-paragraph obituary. Such effort makes for quick reading but fails to present the complex detailing, multiple contradictions, and rich texture that form the real substance of everyday lives. Nor was my childhood "done" to me. I was not a victim of my father's anger, my peers' harassment and violence, or my sister's jealous rage, as I have told myself I was at other times of my life. Despite the constrictions placed on children—owing to economic dependence, patriarchal regulations, and the dictatorial governing style of most families and most classrooms—children are always to a greater or lesser extent active agents in participating in the production of their own childhoods and adolescences (James and Prout 1990; Mayall 1994). Although as children we do not necessarily ask for what we get, neither do most of us passively accept our circumstances. If the culture does not offer us opportunities to physically remove ourselves from sites of persecution or deprivation, then many of us find ways to remove ourselves emotionally and transport ourselves psychically to other worlds. We play an active role in shaping our own consciousnesses, creating our values, and invoking our own spiritual resources. This is as true for most children as it is for most adults.

There is much that needs to be said in favor of transforming the economic, political, and social position of children in the United States and in removing key structural barriers to the health and wellness of all children. Were there a major movement to democratize the family, shift from nuclear family structures to the communal raising of children, or economically emancipate children from dependence on their parents, we might radically transform the life chances of children of all races as well as the landscape of social problems that emerge from the squalid contemporary conditions of childhood. Suppose that we were to guarantee all children over the age of, say, ten years not only shelter, schooling, and proper nutrition but the right to determine where and with whom they lived, the freedom of self-expression and self-determination, and the right to full participation in the institutions of our democracy. If we were to do so, we might find that we had created the circumstances that would deliver to our culture an adult populace more capable of managing their day-to-day lives, less likely to engage in abusive power relations with others, and ultimately more capable of participating responsibly in the processes of democratic citizenship.

The abuses of power foisted on children in the name of "child protection," "child defense," or "child welfare" may be well-intended attempts to offer care and sustenance, but they do little to displace a construction and lived reality of childhood that do their best to leave a significant portion of our population economically dependent, socially isolated, and politically disenfranchised. The first experience that all Americans have toward understanding inequality, oppression, and disempowerment may be rooted in our culture's treatment of children. What is done to children and what they learn from these power dynamics provide a model for the lifelong misuse of power and play a shaping role in a range of inequities with which our culture struggles. The original template for our contemporary systems of racism and sexism is the adult–child paradigm that dominates the first two decades of most Americans' lives. In contemporary America, the original sin is the symbolic and embodied violence structured into our concept of childhood and the ways we organize children's lives. Ageism, rarely seriously considered or deconstructed, inculcates all of us into the powerful paradigm of oppression.

I am not talking here about the child who is beaten regularly by a parent, chained to a bed, and forced to lie in his or her own excrement. When one talks about the abuse of children, we conjure up visions of frail waifs with bruises on their bodies, boys who are regularly locked in closets without food, girls who are repeatedly sexually violated by fathers. All these are horrible conditions and must be addressed. Yet there is another level of abuse perpetrated against children and youth, one that is experienced by so-called normal kids who function in their families, schools, and neighborhoods, seemingly without any problems. This form of abuse, while more subtle, is about the misuse of personal and institutional power; it is rooted in simple-minded concepts of childhood that make us see these small people as incapable, inept, and profoundly dependent. It allows adults to smugly believe that children's supposed inexperience demands that we direct, monitor, and control every aspect of their daily lives.

An entire apparatus has been put in place that ensures the perpetuation of this adult–child power dynamic and that works from infancy through young adulthood to immerse young people into social worlds that treat them much the way women were treated before feminism, as blacks were treated before emancipation and, again, before the civil rights movement: as hysterical, immature, know-nothings, who are not capable of full participation in the institutions of our democracy. The science of developmentalism and most of the theories in the educational psychology canon serve as the foundation for a range of social institutions that function to suppress, repress, and incarcerate childhood. Adult–child relationships emerge from that context. The books that instruct parents in the raising of children; the folk wisdom passed down by grandparents; the social networks of other parents sharing their experiences with discipline, behavior problems, and children's insubordination are all woven together to produce the social fabric that puts children in their place. Schools, Disney cartoons, youth activities, summer camps all play a role in perpetuating the inequities of the child–adult system.

The oppression of children and youth constitutes the foundation out of which highly charged issues related to LGBT and gender-nonconforming youth arise. It was not my father's belt repeatedly hitting my butt that wreaked havoc on my childhood; it was the fact that no social institutions provided me with resources to compensate for the physical differences between an eight-year-old boy and a thirty-five-year-old man. Were he striking another thirty-five-year-old man, there would be legal statutes, social rules, and cultural processes that offer options for response. Because I was a person who was eight years old and legally regarded as his property, I had no recourse in the law at that time. More so, I had no cultural models of children fighting back, no access to education about my rights, no use of lawyers, and no self-defense materials such as Mace. Rather than being *born* vulnerable, as people like to think of children, social and cultural forces colluded to *make* me vulnerable.

It was not the bully taunting me with names such as "sissy" and "faggot" that made me feel hemmed in, cornered, and without alternatives; it was the fact that I was required to be present in the social institution of schooling every day and that the education system offered me no choice of school, no end in sight for schooling, and no opportunities to confront my persecutors in a democratic forum. While I would lie in bed at night and fantasize violent schemes that would ensure the death or public humiliation of the boys who tormented me, I had neither the resources nor inclination to enact my fantasies in real life. There were no children's courts in which I could confront my tormentors, and complaints to my teachers or parents led me to be derided as a tattletale.

When I read about adolescent students who bring shotguns to school, I do not share in the shock and surprise of many of my colleagues. Instead I feel a powerful recognition: *this could have been me*. If some children experience years of soul-numbing persecution, if they are offered no comfort, no support, no court in which to confront and win compensation from perpetrators, then who is ultimately healthier—the children who are empowered enough to strike back or those who take no action and self-destruct?

By saying this, I do not intend to excuse the increasing numbers of outcasts, misfits, geeks, and queers who explode into violence in their school cafeterias and shoot willy-nilly in all directions, striking down students and teachers with whom they have no complaint. At the same time, I find myself wondering whether these enraged students were actually targeting the bullies who made their lives miserable for years. In my own childhood fantasies of revenge, that is precisely what I did.

If we ever hope to eliminate the horrors visited on young people, we cannot do it solely by initiating superficial violence-prevention programs or peer education workshops about child abuse and neglect. We have got to face the core issues head-on. Not only does this involve providing young people with the legal status, knowledge, and resources to be fully empowered human beings with the power and authority of self-determination, but it also means finding ways to radically transform what we believe is the nature of childhood in America and reduce the privileges and stature awarded to adults due solely to their biological ages.

BEYOND NATURE VERSUS NURTURE: TOWARD A VOLITIONAL UNDERSTANDING OF SEXUAL IDENTITY

This book is about me. It is about the young boy who found ways to explore his own body and others' in the bathtub, in backyard tree houses, and behind closed doors. It is about the boy's eyes that rebelliously gazed at his mother's fingers, neck, and breasts; looked at body parts on beaches; and became transfixed on his father's body hair when they showered together. It is about that boy's hands that, despite classroom lessons that attempted to desexualize childhood, boldly explored his young body, seeking sources of pleasure and release. It is about the central role of pleasure in the lives of all people, including children, and the risks we will take because we enjoy feeling good. It is about the belief many of us hold—including many children—that we deserve pleasure and happiness, the enjoyment of picking our noses, the thrill of hugging our security blankets, the excitement we find in fondling our genitals, the satisfaction we garner by stealing cookies from the cookie jar.

This book is about the young adolescent whose erotic obsession suddenly changed as he directed his gaze from newspaper cartoon character Brenda Starr's cleavage to her exotic and elusive paramour Basil St. John. It is about how he charged boys who performed traditional masculinities—athletes, hoods, surfer boys, and even bullies—with intense erotic power. It is about how he claimed taboo desires by selectively paging through teen-idol magazines, muscle magazines, and the male swimsuit advertisements relegated to the back pages of his father's *Playboy* magazines. It is about how deviating from the norm brought not only confusion and fear but also comfort, joy, and a sense of personal triumph.

I do not believe that I was born gay, just as I was not born effeminate, gentle, or gender nonconforming, even though the limited ways in which we understand the role of biology, genetics, and conscious choice make it seem as though people are born homo- or heterosexual, gender conforming or not. Instead, I believe that I was born as most other mammals are—that is, sexual and capable of erotically responding to a range of stimuli: touches, words, smells, sounds, emotions, foods, pets, symbolic images. My turn toward boys and men during my early adolescence was not a genetically determined act; it was a utilitarian act rooted in a kind of personal choice that lies below the level of consciousness. I never cognitively opted to instill special meaning into my relationships with boys and men. At the same time, I cannot claim that I failed to receive the clear and powerful message from society that such attractions were sick, sinful, or criminal. I knew the social meaning of being queer, just as all boys of my generation knew it. Nevertheless, I chose to invest my friendships with boys and men a special meaning, a spiritual power that I rarely conferred on girls or women. In a world where homosexuality was not spoken about and where gay people were derided, I made the decision to love men. While some might see this as a product of a gay gene or as an act of self-destruction, I see it as a profound act of courage and rebellion. Becoming queer was the best thing I ever did for myself.

Our culture is terribly confused about questions of individual agency. Is it any wonder? We grow up receiving ambiguous messages about a range of matters related to cognitive decision making, individual choice, and the process of drawing distinctions and charting preferences. What made me opt for vanilla over chocolate ice cream during my childhood? I understood it at the time as a simple matter determined by the biology of my taste buds. How did I come to read all of the Oz books, when my parents would have preferred me to become an enthusiastic reader of Tom Swift or the Hardy Boys? Even these days, when I'm called on to explain my preferences for eating Thai food, listening to country music, watching *The West Wing*, or driving pickup trucks, my initial reaction is to simply state, "They just appeal to me." Yet sociologist Pierre Bourdieu's work (1982, 1984) has shown how even seemingly meaningless distinctions and simple preferences may be laden with values and with complex meanings as well as political meanings.

I have come to view sexual preferences, including the sex(es) of one's chosen partners, as I view all preferences, through a Bourdieuian lens. Nothing in my genetic makeup predetermined that I would focus my erotic interest on one sex to the exclusion of the other, and nothing biological within me determined that I would focus on men. Instead, I made a choice that was bold and transgressive—a type of choice that occurs below the level of consciousness but is as closely linked to volition as those made by conscious decision-making processes. While I initially understood this choice to involve a preference and attraction to certain tropes of masculinity—facial and body hair; a deep, resonant voice; the musculature of male bodies—I believe now that such attractions extended deeper. As my friendships and comfortable relationships were with girls and other gender-nonconforming boys, I chose to expand the landscape of my world by focusing my attractions on boys and men who embraced traditional forms of masculinity.

I never made a cognitive decision to separate myself from girls and women; in fact, my adult life has always included the same close friendships and joyous sharings as I had with females during my childhood. I have never been separated from the values and cultures of diverse female social worlds. In fact, many gay men will tell you that even in an all-male gay bar, the feminine is never far away. I can be a big man and a big girl.

I talk through my history here to recommend that we consider thinking of LGBT youth as a group that has chosen, on some level, to direct their erotic energies in directions that the culture at large abhors. In a democracy supposedly founded on some level of respect for individual freedom, such choices cut to the core of our civic values and are part and parcel of the spirit of democracy. All of us—including children and youth—should have the right to organize our gender, sex, and intimate relationships in consensual ways that we find satisfying and congruent with principles by which we choose to live. If we are capable of regarding queer youth as having the volition to choose renegade identities and rupture traditional gender regulations, then we might approach our work with them in more respectful ways. As teachers, parents, and supportive adults, we can take the liberal path and attempt to prevent slurs and protect those who need protection from violence. Rather than do so, however, we can alternately provide queer youth with the understandings, legal rights, and resources to protect themselves and to continue their valuable project of transforming social norms.

QUEER CULTURE, GAY MALE TEACHERS, AND AUTHENTIC CULTURAL DIVERSITY

This book is about me. It is about a man who splits his time during the academic term between living near a small public university amid the redwoods of rural Northern California and living at his home in the Castro neighborhood of San Francisco, perhaps the neighborhood with the highest percentage of gay men in the nation. It is about an openly gay professor on a liberal campus where gay issues seem to never have been a central matter for public discussion. It is about a professor whose academic work focuses on preparing candidates to become elementary school teachers and whose political efforts focus on gay men's health activism and sexual liberation.

Identity management issues have followed me throughout my career, sometimes stalking me obsessively, like a slasher in a 1950s suspense movie. Early in my career, when I was a sixth-grade teacher, I remained closeted and pursued my activist work discreetly. I employed pseudonyms when I wrote for local gay newspapers. After two years, I lost that job when I came out as a gay man to the school's principal (see Rofes 1985). Much to my surprise, I was soon hired as a middle school teacher by an independent progressive school nearby. In 1978, I became the first openly gay schoolteacher in Massachusetts.

While teaching at that school, I worked evenings to establish some of the initial programs for LGBT youth, and I founded Boston's first organization for lesbian and gay schoolteachers. During these years, in the late 1970s and early 1980s, I often found myself in the spotlight, speaking out on gay issues and schools to an uninformed media, to hostile public officials, and to concerned groups of parents. I cautiously put forward a public identity of what I thought would be a respectable gay man. I appeared traditionally masculine, muzzled my radical politics, and I presented my relationship with my lover as if we were a traditional monogamous couple. I could bring my teacher identity with my gay male identity only by cleansing the gay identity of all aspects of gender trouble or sexual rebellion. I believed that my being homosexual was enough; to be queer as well would simply be too much for the public to handle.

I left my career as a schoolteacher in the mid-1980s when I felt compelled to become more closely involved in AIDS and gay community organizing. I moved to California, throwing myself into the tumult of the movement, and I worked full-time in gay and AIDS organizations. In some ways, I left my schoolteacher identity behind during these years and took on a heightened public presence as a gay activist.

These were daring and frightening times. I had expected that the move away from children would allow me to maintain more integrity in my public gay identity, but I instead found that working at a gay nonprofit or leading an AIDS service organization presented its own identity management challenges, too. Was it acceptable for the director of the gay and lesbian community center to show up at the local leather bar wearing a harness and set of chaps? When most of the gay men in San Francisco were clients, volunteers, or staff members of the AIDS organization at which I worked, was it appropriate for me to enjoy myself at a local sex club in full view of some of the organization's clients or board members? How was it possible to maintain my civil libertarian political views or my perspectives on the sexual rights of adolescents while the board of the gay center at which I worked was refusing to allow members of the local chapter of the North American Man/Boy Love Association—a group whose primary purpose was to create public discussion and debate on the sexual rights of young people—to meet in our building?

Many gay men appear easily able to make compromises related to managing their disparate identities. They seem to find nothing objectionable about enacting traditional masculinities in their work lives and keeping their private lives private. They are content to save their camping and pigging for after hours. Not me. Early readings of feminist literature heightened my awareness of the politics lurking behind such starkly divided boundaries. I learned from lesbian–feminist writers such as Adrienne Rich, Dorothy Allison, Jewelle Gomez, Amber Hollibaugh, Pat Califia, Cherie Moraga, Gayle Rubin, and Joan Nestle what violence is visited on our souls through secrets and silences. Why is it acceptable for employees to share all-American stories about family barbecues and attending hockey games, whereas narratives about attending full-moon orgies or Halloween drag contests are seen as inappropriate? Why do public gay male figures present themselves as either happily ensconced in a monogamous marriage or forced into a life of martyred celibacy ("I work *all* the time")? In a democracy, people should have the right to organize their relationship to sex, fidelity, and gender however they choose.

After years of struggle and soul-searching, I maintain little shame about my erotic desires or practices. Pretending that all relationships are structured as Ozzie and Harriet's are does a disservice to those people of various sexual identities who have organized their emotions, desires, and relationships in other ways. This pretense does a tremendous disservice to the notion of liberty.

Ultimately, for me, this book struggles to address questions that I have struggled with my entire adult life, ones focused on cultural integrity, pluralism, and participatory democracy—concepts central to the work of elementary school teachers in the United States today. The assimilationist notion encourages us to embrace a process whereby all Americans jump into the stewpot: as the heat is turned up to simmer, the rough edges get melted away and we are left with one thick, creamy ooze. We aim for the Chicano kindergartener to closely resemble Anglo children in learning styles, peer relations, and communication patterns by the sixth grade. We admire the deaf child who seems "normal." Although we tell ourselves that this stewpot process alters all children, in reality, the process of assimilation is ultimately about subjugated populations coming to resemble dominant group norms. At best, mainstream America develops an appreciation for Thai food or hip-hop music but remains ignorant of the history of the Hmong people or the social and economic forces that force people into poverty.

For gay men, this melting-pot model offers us cultural acceptance in exchange for eliminating all the ways in which our bodies, lives, and kinship patterns differ from traditional heteromasculinities. Congressman Barney Frank can be accepted as a mainstream political leader today because he has succeeded in relegating his use of call boys to the distant past, packaging such activities as unfortunate episodes linked to the perils of the closet. His credibility as a public figure would likely be diminished if he continued to employ the services of escorts and did so without secrets or shame. Even if such practices were not illegal, such brazen violations of heteronorms would bring banishment from the corridors of power and would diminish one's respect in the public sphere. Witness George Michael, caught cruising in a men's room in Beverly Hills, who responded without guilt and who exhibited an awareness and appreciation for gay male cultural norms, rarely exhibited by big-name celebrities. The recording artist's refusal to be shamed into a narrative of regret, claims of sexual addiction, and rhetorical self-flagellation created a public backlash in which his popularity and public image took a hit.

Assimilation has its rewards. I see many children from poor white families who want nothing more than to fit into the commodified consumption patterns of the middle class. We read studies of black children who express preferences for white dolls and of Asian immigrant children who are embarrassed by their parents' use of languages other than English. Likewise, the gay male teen who adheres to traditional gender roles and comes out as captain of the football team is more likely to win support and acclaim from his peers than the queen in the drama club. Because the primary social worlds that children occupy—the family, the neighborhood, the school, the religious institutions—reward assimilation and pathologize difference, is it any wonder that children wrestle with conflicting drives to both resist the norms and embrace them?

Many contemporary gay men exhibit this same powerful desire for assimilation. Many of us have seen the social position of gay issues change remarkably in our lifetimes. Those who are now choosing same-sex relationships and even coming out as LGBT people are those who would never have done so before, during a time when societal approbation, social isolation, and public silence on homosexuality reigned supreme. The shifting position of gay issues creates an entire subbody of unexamined aspects in which the normalization of homosexuality encourages a once-despised population to hunger deeply for public approval. I live with this tendency every day as I find myself enjoying the benefits of being openly gay that I never thought I would see in my lifetime. How effective would I be as a professor if my hands fluttered as I lectured or if I girlishly crossed my legs as I sat in front of my class? Would my lover's family embrace me as warmly as they do if we did not keep some boundaries between their images of us as a couple and the reality of the ways we organize our sex? Would I enjoy domestic-partner airline benefits through the employer of my lover, an airplane mechanic, if the company knew we were nonmonogamous? I hope so, but I, too, play this game of assimilation and public performance because I want the rewards.

The stewpot model of cultural assimilation requires all of us to strip away our differences and eliminate any attribute that conflicts with the status quo. We enter public sphere denuded of any special qualities that might be judged as problematic, confusing, or threatening to the existing structures of power and privilege. At the same time, another model of cultural diversity affirms differences and does not demand that rough edges be eliminated or that distinctions be expunged. Under this model, individuals and groups continue to maintain and value key differences from the dominant culture—differences in style, values, social practices, histories, and worldviews—and move into the mainstream unabashedly, holding these differences intact. People enter the workplace and the public sphere, bringing their original cultures and ways of being: the work at hand is then to learn to work across lines of authentic difference.

Under a truly multicultural model of diversity, our collective project is to work together, drawing strength from the ways in which we are similar as well as the ways in which we are different. It is about resisting a trigger reaction of fear when we are placed next to someone different from us, and it is about cultivating an interest and appreciation for that difference. There is a huge distinction between a multiculturalism that respects cultural integrity and challenges us to work across cultural differences and an assimilationism that asks us to deny, mitigate, or vanish the differences. It is the distinction between saying that "I don't see race; I only see people" and saying that "my students come from many different cultural backgrounds and I will work with them best if I gain an appreciation for their home cultures."

For gay men who identify with an urban gay culture characterized by a heightened attention to gender performance and gender play, to patterns of kinship traced through friendship networks rather than through nuclear families, and to an innovative and daring relationship to our bodies and desires, the tug between cultural integrity and assimilation is strong. Whereas some imagine gay men's kinship patterns and sexual cultures as unfortunate products of homophobia and antigay laws, I believe that these patterns will continue to thrive, even as the bulwark of homophobia subsides. They will continue because many gay men truly do find pleasure and meaning in our cultural forms of social organization and sexual networks. They will continue because we are willing to make sacrifices in our pubic lives and in our work lives, but not in our private lives and not in our lives in community with other gay men.

Are teachers sexual beings? One wouldn't think so by visiting an elementary school, by reviewing the curriculum of teacher preparatory programs, or by attending a conference of LGBT educators. Especially at the elementary school level, teachers who present themselves with even a hint of the erotic are shunned. I have noticed that the discussion of maintaining "proper classroom appearance" that occurs between my credential students and the mentor teachers, university supervisors, and principals with whom they interact is as much about desexing the teacher's body as it is about up-classing it. Once again, white middle-class patriarchal norms rule supreme.

In some places, the sexuality of teachers becomes exposed. Certainly grabbing headlines are those public scandals involving teacher–student sexual conduct and male teachers arrested on moral charges for having sex in public parks and rest stops. The position of sex at the high school level is distinct from that at the elementary schools. The television show *Boston Public*, focusing on life inside an urban high school, is rife with romances and philandering among teachers at the school and between teachers and students; it effectively captures, perhaps with a bit of exaggeration, the issues faced in many high schools. Likewise, anyone who imagines schoolteachers as eunuchs only needs to hang around the hotel bar during one of the major teacher conferences. Teachers are clearly sexual beings, but teacher culture has evolved in a desexed way.

Is it possible to allow teachers to present themselves as full human beings, including as sexual beings, without harassing or violating their students? Can we unabashedly hold our sexuality around students of any age in a way that is neither violating or predatory? In a world where many young people have been subjected to sexual harassment, coercion, and assault, is a gesture toward a sexualized teacher simply going to push buttons that need not be pushed? Or could a reasonable integration of one's erotic nature into one's teacher identity help students gain greater agency over their own sexualities? These are questions I struggle with as a professor, just as I struggled with them years ago as a sixth-grade teacher.

STATUS QUO OR STATUS QUEER? A RADICAL APPROACH TO EDUCATION, SEXUALITY, AND SCHOOLING

After thirty years of increasingly concerted efforts to improve the experience of lesbian, gay, bisexual, transgendered, and gender-nonconforming youth in schools, why does it seem today as if homophobic and gender-based persecution among young people is at an all-time high? If the United States has had openly lesbian, gay, and bisexual teachers working in schools for the past three decades, why does it seem as if educators continue to be marginalized, harassed, terminated, and hounded out of jobs when they make the transition from being covertly to overtly homosexual? How can the media saturate America with things gay while the formal processes and sites of K–12 schooling continue, with rare exception, to remain silent on gay issues?

This book tries to answer these questions by examining critical contemporary issues linking sexuality, education, and schooling: books for children of lesbian and gay parents; the influence of queer teachers on their students; the various approaches to antigay harassment; the relationship between teachers and controversial issues such as sex and gender; gay men's shifting relationship to HIV education; and the cultural politics fueling debates around gay issues in schools. As the national battle for equal rights for LGBT people targeted traditional American institutions in the 1990s—namely, the military and marriage—gay inclusion in public education emerged as a central battleground in local communities throughout the country. Although liberal Americans have begun to embrace gay rights as a critical component on their political agenda, it is unclear whether the hiring of openly gay men as kindergarten teachers or the affirmation of lesbian-identified seventh graders are included as priorities. It also remains unclear whether queers are invited to join in the sites of public education on their own terms.

This book takes seriously the powerful right-wing forces that have emerged locally and nationally to resist the integration of gay people into public schooling. Yet its central argument does not focus on the traditional opponents of gay rights—religious fundamentalists, socially conservative

Republicans, and the Catholic Church. This book argues instead that the collective efforts of LGBT people and their justice-minded allies to combat homophobia and heterosexism in schools have served to buttress a system where power functions to oppress and marginalize entire groups and strengthen precisely those forces that ignite social tensions and continually reproduce inequality.

How can this be? When we began our work to make schools safe for gay people in the 1970s, our intentions were good. We saw ourselves as part of a broader movement to protect the rights and the stature of all educators and to promote full inclusion of all children and youth in public education—kids of color, special education students, and incipient dropouts from poor families. As we went about coming out in our classrooms and teacher unions, organizing gay youth programs, and demanding that school libraries diversify their offerings on gay issues, we understood that for public schools to be truly public, all members of society had a right to participate. This impelled us to break through barriers to the hiring or retention of lesbian and gay teachers by gaining union support, winning contract protections, and educating parents and school committees. It moved us to make our schools safer for LGBT teens and gender-nonconforming children and to put a halt to the assumption that all our students are situated in families where there is a father and a mother.

In the late 1970s and early 1980s, I embraced the movement for full inclusion of all children and all teachers in American schools. It led me to initiate the formation of Boston Area Gay and Lesbian Schoolworkers, one of the first organizations of queer teachers in the nation, and to begin providing peer support to closeted queer teachers as we as a community began to make initial interventions in the policy arena. At twenty-three, I was motivated to begin Out There and Committee for Gay Youth, summer programs for gay and lesbian teens, ages fifteen to nineteen, which eventually grew into Boston Area Gay and Lesbian Youth, one of the pioneering queer youth organizations in the nation. By the age of thirty, when I became executive director of the Los Angeles Gay and Lesbian Community Center, I was overseeing the nation's largest gay youth program, including over a dozen peer-support groups throughout Los Angeles County, two shelters for homeless youth, and one of the first HIV-prevention programs aimed at gay male youth. When I discuss the first stage of work on gay issues in schools throughout this book, I want to be clear that I am pointing the finger not only at the work of others but at my own work as well. This volume is as much a reflection on the shortcomings of my own work as it is of the field at large. It represents a midlife rethinking of work that we have been engaged in for thirty years.

While much progress remains to be made, we have done an excellent job in beginning to address homophobia and antigay bigotry. At the same time, we have failed to confront a more ominous challenge—the root causes for these inequities. What is it about our current system of schooling that produces the conditions in which bullies thrive? How do the ways we conceptualize, recruit, and prepare teachers create conditions in which a system that oppressively categorizes, sorts, and assigns young people is perpetuated and strengthened? How does the contemporary position of children and youth in our culture serve to drive scapegoating, harassment, and persecution? Is much of our work on gay issues in schools ultimately focused on assimilation and reform, rather than on authentic cultural pluralism and radical social change?

In this book, I argue that we have done terrific work in creating first-stage approaches to a range of policy matters related to queers and education but that such approaches are inadequate to bring about the deep and profound change needed to transform systems of education in our nation. The book proposes that we move toward a second stage of work that digs to the root cause of these social problems. For me, the change proposed in this book exemplifies the distinction between liberal approaches to social problems and radical approaches. Liberal approaches focus on additive approaches, on tinkering, and on gradual shifts; yet, they leave the overarching systems and regimes of power and privilege firmly in place. Radical approaches believe something fundamental needs to be transformed for authentic and sweeping changes to occur.

I believe that the greatest challenge we face in school reform involves the radical transformation of our foundational assumptions about children, youth, and teachers. When historians of education review the past hundred years of schooling in America, their major finding usually focuses on the relative imperviousness of the classroom to innovation and change, and they cite many social and economic forces that contribute to the failure to transform school and classroom practice (Cuban 1995; Tyack 1974). Yet I have yet to see any educational historian, sociologist, or anthropologist link the stability of school structures to the stability of our conceptions of childhood. Despite the significant work over the past fifty years that has examined the ways in which our assumptions and understanding of childhood are linked to profound imbalances of power and privilege, our work in schools continues to leave this matter fully unexamined. If we hope to transform schools and classrooms, we must take the leap, radically transform our cultural understandings of children and youth, and examine the implications for our systems of education.

To achieve this, we must eliminate systems of power that effectively trigger a cycle of domination and abuse, an endless craving for repeated social ranking, and a culture rife with overt force, subtle coercion, and widespread disenfranchisement. We all like to say that we seek to "empower" children, but our efforts occur within a system of public education that is structured to do otherwise. What do we truly mean by "democracy" or "empowerment"?

Are we willing to stand by while empowered young people make decisions we consider unwise? Is it possible for adults to facilitate the empowerment of children and youth without giving up power themselves? If we are willing to deconstruct and transform our cultural understandings of childhood, are we willing to do likewise with adulthood?

By failing to understand the ways in which unethical uses of authority and power serve to acculturate young people into nonconsensual rituals of dominance and submission and to socialize them into pecking-order systems, we remain blind to the betrayal of our youth. When addressing antigay remarks in the classroom, we demand that teachers intervene and punish; hence, we strengthen in a Foucaultian sense the very same system of surveillance, regulation, judgment, castigation, and correction that consistently imposes adult authority on children and youth. We produce and advocate for "inclusive" literature in libraries, which results in the simple queerification of texts that continue to depict young people as innocent, vulnerable, and dependent on adult supervision. In our attempts to win inclusion of openly gay and lesbian teachers, we insist that they serve as exemplary role models, and then we strip them of anything that might spur controversy, influence their students' emerging identities, or catalyze radical change. These are hardly strategies for empowerment.

I have recently argued that the one useful response to today's teacher shortage is to expand sites of recruitment to places as yet untouched by teacher recruitment drives: state prisons, homeless shelters, gay bars, and blighted urban neighborhoods. At first I made this suggestion ironically, but as I had time to reflect on the challenges we face in recruiting teachers committed to social change rather than in reproducing the status quo, I have come to consider this strategy more seriously. If we are trying to shift our system of public education away from its role as a reproducer of social inequities, then we need teachers who are willing to challenge the status quo. Better yet, we need teachers with experience in challenging the status quo. Those who survive on the margins of society acquire an intense experience of being the outsider. These outlaws and social misfits may be more likely to advocate for the radical transformation of ideologies and for the dramatic restructuring of systems of education than are the traditional pool of people whom we cycle through teacher preparation programs.

What would our schools look like if their faculties were comprised of ex-cons, queers, and street people? How might the life chances of all children be different were there more welfare mothers working as elementary educators? If we filled our classrooms with people with heightened experiences of resisting and countering abuse, victimization, marginalization, and approbation, would we succeed at moving school closer to our social justice aims than if we continued to hire all the Miss Jean Brodys and Jaime Escalantes of the world?

As a culture, we tell ourselves how much we love children and how committed we are to protecting them from savage forces and menacing threats. At the same time, by seeing children and youth as innocent and vulnerable, we participate in the creation of structures and social forces that keep children from information, resources, social organization, and self-concepts that might allow them to produce themselves as strong, savvy people. This is profoundly political; it is about power, and it is about adult fears of children with power. It is about the political manipulation of children for the benefit of adults. I understand it as mass political abuse of children, writ large.

This book is the culmination of thirty years spent teaching, organizing, researching, and writing about LGBT issues in schools and struggling now to critically rethink our baseline assumptions about sexuality, education, and schooling. At its core, it argues that it is possible for educators—not only LGBT educators but all social justice–minded educators—to change the world for young people, not only queer youth, but all youth. Making deep and meaningful change requires us to face head-on the barriers in our path and the work that needs to be done. It requires us to critically challenge our core beliefs and the categories we utilize in our work, and it urges us to consider what radical visions of queerness might offer our debates about education and schooling. It calls on all educators who are committed to social justice to radically rethink our efforts and our role in either maintaining or radically transforming the status quo.

2

Candy from Strangers: Queer Teachers and the (Im)Moral Development of Children

As I sifted through my pile of postal mail today, I came across an envelope with the return address of a student I had taught twenty years ago in a school located in a city three thousand miles away from where I now live. The envelope's style and bulk led me to wonder if it contained a wedding invitation, birth announcement, or news of some other special occasion. After slicing through the paper, sure enough, I found myself reading the announcement of this former student's upcoming nuptials. Immediately I wondered what Andy might be like as a grown man. While he is imprinted in my mind's eye as a short, skinny eleven-year-old boy, I wondered if I would recognize him as a thirty-something adult. Was he still enamored with technology? Did he still listen to awful heavy metal music? Did he ever grow taller than five feet?

One of the long-lasting joys that have come to me as a former school-teacher is watching students grow from childhood through adolescence and into adulthood. Perhaps because I am not a parent, unanticipated visits or communications from former students who are now adults call up a range of powerful feelings. For the largest segment of my tenure as a classroom teacher, I was situated in a mixed-age classroom combining sixth-, seventh-, and eighth-grade students. Working with children throughout this particular three-year period and working with their families as they struggled to bring a child through what is seen in America as the difficult middle school years engages a level of commitment and a depth of intimacy that promote ongoing relationships with many students.

My relationship with these students is also special because I shared with them a particularly difficult moment in my life. After losing a job as a sixth-grade teacher in a nearby suburb because I came out as a gay man, I never thought I would again find a teaching position. Yet, just a few months later, I was hired by a politically progressive independent school in Cambridge, Massachusetts, to revitalize their small, problematic middle school program. In addition to the substantial grunt work associated with managing a classroom, I carried the dubious distinction of being an openly gay K–12 schoolteacher in New England during these critical years for the gay and lesbian movement (1978–1983), and I was one of the only queer educators in our area willing to be openly gay in the media.

Much of the debate about queer teachers during that era centered on a single narrow question: Would the lesbian, gay, or bisexual teacher influence their young students' emerging sexuality? For the most part, we were not asked about our skills as teachers, and few people inquired about our content knowledge and the subjects that we taught. People wanted to know if we would influence impressionable youngsters. This concern was especially pressing in the elementary grades and in middle school, the periods in which, many people believe, students moved toward a specific sexual orientation. These were precisely the matters that were debated at a meeting I attended-with the school board at my previous school, as they considered whether I should be retained or let go as a teacher. This line of inquiry was tightly linked to people's preexisting concept of childhood as a period in which young people are blank slates, vulnerable to outside influences. Some might imagine that a popular and powerful sixth-grade teacher would, without conscious effort or a clear agenda, steer his students toward homosexuality.

Once I was hired as an openly gay sixth- through eighth-grade teacher, I remember in fragmented ways the various times in which my openness with my gay identity interacted with my middle school students. Each fall, I would find an excuse to formally tell my students that I was gay, because I felt uncomfortable raising the matter without a context. Because I was a local activist on gay issues, these announcements usually came around the time I was slated to appear on a television talk show or on the evening news. Rather than have my students learn about my homosexuality from an outside source, I believed that it was appropriate to tell them myself and to answer their questions. During the first few times that I made the announcement, I was filled with anxiety, but after a few years of being an openly gay teacher, I found myself relaxed, more casual about the news than anything else. Because of the school's liberal educational philosophy and the cultural residue of the 1960s, which still enveloped Cambridge during these years, I had few problems inside the school.

It is important to emphasize that my students could be considered "preselected" to respond to my homosexuality with liberal views. As I taught these students during the onset of the conservative entrenchment initiated by President Reagan, these children were situated in Massachusetts, not Orange

County, California, or Little Rock, Arkansas. Their families tended to represent populations that were atypical in the United States at that time: former 1960s activists and counterculture hippies, experimental educators, Harvard professors, grassroots social justice activists, and liberal intellectuals. These were the same populations that made Cambridge a stronghold for progressive social policies such as rent control, child care, affirmative action, and food cooperatives.

Yet some local tensions simmered just below the surface, pitting the former hippies and political progressives against more conservative forces. The surrounding neighborhood's reaction to a school with a gay teacher was quite different from that of parents with children in the school. During this period, urban centers were just beginning to acknowledge that organized communities of gay men and lesbians were in their midst. It was during this particular moment that my coming out as an openly gay teacher in an independent urban school raised issues that I had not anticipated. More than once, I heard from parents that my students—because they had a gay teacher—were being mocked and derided by neighborhood children or were being made fun of at sporting events. No matter how liberal our school was, at the end of each day my students went home to a range of neighborhoods in Cambridge, Boston, Charlestown, Somerville, Malden, and other cities in the metropolitan area—most of which were just beginning to come to terms with the existence of sizable gay communities.

I heard that our school's name, Fayerweather, had been transformed into "Fairy-weather" among the local children who attended public and parochial schools in the neighborhood. It hurt and bothered me that my charges, through no fault of their own, were put in the position of being stigmatized or having to defend their teacher's sexual orientation, but I didn't know if alternatives existed. When I arrived at school one Monday morning and saw the word *FAGGOT* painted graffiti-like over the front of the three-story school building, I could no longer avoid facing that what I saw as a civil rights issue—my right to teach children regardless of my sexual orientation—was experienced as a safety issue or a peer-group issue for my students. Hence, the question concerning the ways a homosexual teacher might influence his students' lives was broadened for us at the Fayerweather school, as we came to understand that in the eyes of a hostile public, simple association with an openly gay person somehow queered the entire school and the entire student body.

This chapter focuses on findings from a survey taken by my former middle school students of Fayerweather Street School, in Cambridge, Massachusetts, long after they had had me as a teacher. The survey's questions focused on their thoughts about the experience of having an openly gay schoolteacher during their middle school years and on the long-term impact of having had a gay teacher as a child. At the time of the survey, they were in their late twenties and early thirties. My former students responded to a range of questions related to their everyday lives as young adolescents who had a teacher with a stigmatized identity during a contentious moment in the struggle for gay and lesbian rights.

I engaged in an extensive search process, attempting to identify, locate, and communicate with former students to persuade them to participate in this study and fill out the survey. This chapter includes the responses of the eleven former students who returned the survey after the first and second rounds of outreach (I taught ninety-four different students during those five years). I certainly do not pretend this is a comprehensive or representative sample. Instead, my aim here is to present a sense of these young men and women's thinking about having had an openly gay teacher twenty years ago, during a time when the social position of homosexuality was vastly different from what it is today. How do they feel having had a gay teacher influenced them? What do they remember about being a sixth, seventh, or eighth grader and having a gay teacher? What did they know about gay issues before they came to my classroom, and how did my class transform their understanding of these controversial matters? Do they think having a gay teacher affected their development in any way? While we now have a significant amount of data that gives voice to openly gay, lesbian, and bisexual educators (Jennings 1994b; Khayatt 1992; Kissen 1996; Rensenbrink 1996), students (Hale and Donahue 1997; Peterfreund and Cheadle 1996; Remafedi 1992), and parents (Casper et al. 1996), this research may be the first to allow students of a so-called social experiment to reflect on the experience using two decades' worth of hindsight.

The respondents include five women and six men, all white and all between the ages of twenty-nine and thirty-two. All eleven respondents identify as heterosexual. Four of the women are married, as are two of the men. One woman and one man are in an unmarried, live-in relationship—ironically (to me, at least) with each other. Six respondents live in the Greater Boston area with five in New York City, Maine, Vermont, Montana, and Australia. Each holds a job within a range of work: park ranger, outdoor educator, songwriter/producer, academician, martial arts teacher, dancer/performance artist, freelance illustrator, software engineer, university development officer, securities partnership tax practitioner, and furniture artist.

This chapter should not be read in any way as a definitive statement on the long-range impact of having a gay teacher on children. Instead, it looks at a small sample of adult heterosexuals who had at least one openly gay teacher during their middle school experience. The chapter provides insights into the ways in which these heterosexual men and women remember the experience of having an openly gay teacher and how that experience influenced their adolescent lives. It begins to answer the question of how queer teachers might influence their students.

When I was in the heat of debates regarding gay schoolteacher issues and was asked about my possible influence on children, I provided what has become the standard liberal answer to the question: "Sexual orientation is determined well before a child enters sixth grade. Teachers do not have the power to influence a student to be gay. If that were the case, then I'd certainly be straight." Fellow queer teachers and I would often roll our eyes at the very idea that queer teachers might influence a child in any way. One friend of mine used to say, "I went to Catholic schools for my entire K–12 education, and I didn't grow up to be a nun!" If conservatives would voice concerns about a teacher's potential influence, we would act as if they were speaking from the Dark Ages and were totally ignorant of current research into sexual development. We would occasionally act affronted, as if they were suggesting that we were strangers lurking around neighborhood playgrounds with bags of candy, ready to lure the children into homosexuality.

Yet I always maintained my own suspicions. At times I wondered whether making it okay to be gay—politically, socially, culturally—would lead fewer people to close themselves off to erotic relations with members of the same sex. In this way, I did not see queer teachers as "turning" someone gay but instead as creating an environment in which children would not have to repress parts of themselves. I also wondered whether the true influence of teachers such as myself lies less in the area of sexual development and more in the area of moral and social development.

The data in this chapter suggest that openly gay teachers can make a difference in their students lives, a view that is contrary to the claims of many gay and lesbian activists who advocate for the rights of gay teachers: that openly queer teachers do not influence their students. According to those students who responded to the survey, some believed that their years under my tutelage influenced the development of their moral views on homosexuality and their acceptance of human diversity. A few of the students believed that their understanding of and relationship to their own sexuality had been affected by having a gay teacher and by engaging in early discussions of sexual orientation. Yet equally important to me is how my students recalled the childhood experience of having an openly gay teacher. How large did it loom in their lives at the time? Did they find discussions of homosexuality confusing or threatening? In what ways did it alter my interactions with them, and in what ways did it alter their interactions with me?

None of the students in this study turned out to be lesbian, gay, bisexual, transgender, or queer. When asked, "What is your current sexual identity? Relationship status? Do you have children?" all of the respondents answered that they were heterosexual. Laura answered, "Hetero. Married. No kids but a dog." Heather wrote, "I am currently married, heterosexual with a 2½ year old son and another son on the way." Brian answered,

> I'm straight. Steady girlfriend whom I've lived with for about 2 years, herself another former student of Eric's. No children. I do not think having a gay teacher had any influence on these matters.

In answering this question, Max acknowledged his own heterosexuality but suggested a way in which a gay former student's experience might be different from his own:

> I am single and am heterosexual. I don't think having a gay teacher influenced my own sexual identity. However, if I was gay, having a gay teacher would make being gay easier.

The truth is, of the dozens of students that I taught during my years at Fayerweather, I only know of a single student who embraces any of these identities, a bisexual woman (for an essay she wrote about our class trip to *The Rocky Horror Picture Show*, see Strong 1996). My feelings have been mixed about the dearth of queers that apparently emerged from my years at Fayerweather. On the one hand, if there were ever a test case for a gay teacher's powerfully influencing his students' sexual identities, in the mind of the radical Right, this was it. Not only did I teach children during the "impressionable" ages of eleven to thirteen, but I was also the children's lead teacher for three years in a row—sixth, seventh, and eighth grade. And I taught all subjects. So there is a part of me that wants to say, "Aha! See? I rub students' noses in homosexuality and they turn out straight nevertheless! Apparently queer teachers have very little influence on their students' sexual identities!"

At the same time, part of me feels disappointed, even a bit like a failure. Did my openness about my gay identity and my activism in fact discourage my students away from LGBT identities? Did I make homosexuality seem so controversial that any students with the potential to be queer ran in the other direction? By somewhat normalizing queerness, did I rob it of any potential cachet or transgressive appeal?

I don't think I really thought about it much at the time.

My former students offered a range of responses after being asked, "As you look back, what do you remember about being a kid and having a gay teacher? Overall, what kind of experience did you think it was at the time?"

Some recalled wondering what the big deal was all about. Stefanie was a sixth grader who was one of the student representatives on the committee that first hired me at the school. Although I was her primary teacher for the sixth, seventh, and eighth grade, Stefanie was one of those surveyed who asserted that my homosexuality made little difference to her at the time (as did Cheryl's, a lesbian teacher who was part of our middle school team during Stefanie's final year at the school):

> I recall other people, particularly people in the media, making a much bigger deal out of it than I felt it to be. I don't remember Eric or Cheryl's gayness as being the sole, defining aspect of their personalities or my sense of their abilities as teachers.

Ben, a thirty-year-old martial arts instructor in Burlington, Vermont, shared Stefanie's sentiment that, to a young child, having a gay teacher was no big deal:

> I do not have any major memories of Eric as a "gay" teacher, so much as a teacher. I think that his openness about being gay made it more natural, something that was simply another element of himself. . . . Perhaps the most significant memory is a time after school when I walked home with Glen, a fellow student who I thought was rather conservative. I told him that Eric was gay in the same manner than someone mentions that Elvis is still alive—hoping to shock and startle, and perhaps impress him with my erudition. I recall being embarrassed when Eric apparently heard about this, and realized that it was inappropriate to speak of his "gayness" out of context, as something sensational.

Nick, who works as an outdoor educator, shared Ben's perspective, recalling aspects of my teaching persona other than my homosexuality as being more central to his young life. Referring to my homosexuality, Nick captures a child's worldview of that situation: "I don't think I really thought about it much at the time. Eric was a big, intimidating teacher and being scared of conflict with him stands out the most." Max, a twenty-eight-year-old park ranger, responded likewise by noting, "At the time, I don't think I cared that much."

Heather, thirty-three, a tax practitioner and mother of two children, recalled,

> I remember that I was dealing with a number of new issues the year I spent at Fayerweather. The most pressing issue was my parents' impending and volatile divorce, but the open curriculum at the school and spending each day with the first person I ever knew to be gay were also new and challenging experiences for me. The major focus for me that year was myself and how to cope with the divorce. Although not unaware of the fact that Eric was gay, I do not remember at the time that fact having a major impact on me.

For some of the students who responded to the survey, what stood out in their memories was less my gay identity and more my political activism. John, now a twenty-nine-year-old software engineer, wrote,

> I don't think there was anything memorable in terms of the day-to-day impact in the classroom. Eric taught the 3 Rs as well or better than any teacher. What is memorable is that Eric was active in the gay rights movement and his activities would sometimes come up. I think the first time they did was when I was in Jeannie's class [a third-, fourth-, and fifth-grade class] and Eric was on a local TV talk show during lunch and we got to watch it—this was optional. I don't remember this being integrated into the curriculum in any way.

One student, Hannah, thirty-two years old and now a teacher at Fayerweather, also remembered the experience of seeing a teacher on television as an important and memorable event. Hannah recalled students' responding differently to me before and after I came out as a gay man. She wrote,

> I remember when we *suspected* Eric was gay and we joked around about it behind his back, but after he told us, it wasn't funny anymore. There was no more tension around the issue. It became a non-issue. I remember being proud when he was on t.v. about being gay.

Two of the respondents to the survey recalled finding my homosexuality to be significant. Sophie, who at the time was ten years old and the youngest student in the class, recalled considering discussions of my homosexuality as "enlightening, educative, productive of tolerance and respect for differences." In a similar manner, Laura, now a thirty-three-year-old development associate for a university, found discussions about my homosexuality to have an educative impact:

> Looking back in junior high school, I was fascinated with sexuality in general (really, who wasn't?) Anyway, any frank discussion with an adult on the matter was great—demystifying such a powerful topic. It seemed good at the time to be able to discuss homosexuality with an adult.

Any relationship with a sexual component was a bit abstract.

Students offered a number of different responses when asked, "Did you know what 'gay' meant when you were in Eric's class? What did you think then?" Some students' responses situated themselves clearly in the cultural politics of a liberal East Coast city during the 1970s. Stefanie noted,

> I knew what it meant before I was in Eric's class. My parents had colleagues and friends who were gay. I think I only personally knew gay men rather than

women, though. My first discovery of what "gay" meant probably came when I was eight or nine, from older kids in my neighborhood.

Ben shared an experience similar to Stefanie's, being introduced to gay people through his parents who were involved in local progressive community groups:

> I had a very liberal family and my house contained a number of manuscripts and books containing information on sexuality in general and being gay in particular. . . . So homosexuality from an early age was something I understood as being "natural," although I was obviously influenced by the dominant straight culture's often-frightened and negative perception of homosexuality.

Brian, a singer, songwriter, and music producer, similarly did not seem to view having a gay teacher as noteworthy. He wrote,

> To be honest, the experience for me at the time was unremarkable. I didn't give it much thought. I had known openly gay people in my family's circle of friends for as long as I could remember, some of them teachers in other schools I had attended. So this was another instance of a familiar situation to me. . . . I certainly knew what "gay" meant. I did not concern myself with details of gay sexual intimacy, nor do I think I was exposed to much if any information. All I knew was that some people love people of the same sex and that was entirely normal.

Once again, John did not recall considering the experience of having a gay teacher as significant to his early-adolescent self. Responding to questions of whether he knew the meaning of the term "gay" and what he recalls thinking about homosexuality during those years, John wrote,

> Yes, I did [know what "gay" meant]. What did I think then? Mostly about TV, books, friends, and how hard writing is . . . about the notion of being "gay" at that point, any sort of relationship with a sexual component was a bit abstract.

Some students knew what the term "gay" meant before I arrived but found that our talks about my being gay served as a welcome entry into broader discussions of sexuality. As Laura stated,

> I knew what "gay" meant before Eric came out that day but we got to ask questions and benefit from other classmates' questions, so we got to hear stuff we really wanted to know about sex and love.

A few of the students recalled being unclear or uncertain about the meaning of "gay." At least one student did not know what the term "gay" meant before our class discussions that year. Caleb recollected,

I didn't know what "gay" was. I knew some kids used it as a taunt or insult, and I had heard my peers use it without understanding its meaning. I knew "gay" was a bad, mean thing to be called, but I didn't have any idea what it meant to be gay.

Sophie, the ten-year-old who is now a thirty-year-old academic in Australia, "kind of" knew what "gay" meant but added, "I think I learnt what it meant as a result of knowing Eric and due to his openness about his sexuality."

One student responded to this question by explaining that her experience with a gay teacher helped her to clarify what the term "gay" meant. Heather wrote,

Before Eric shared with us that he was gay, I do not remember having had any conversations with people about that topic. I remember at the time telling someone they were "gay" equated to telling them they were stupid. I found it disconcerting that it meant something else entirely and remember catching myself as I used the term in the fashion I was used to. I think the structure of the school allowed for diversity and Eric was a wonderful instructor and friend for all of us during some tough years of our lives. . . . His being gay was always there, but not as much a focus as I would have thought.

In response to the question concerning whether he knew what "gay" meant, Nick recalled, "I did know and had trouble making the sissy stereotype fit on my hulking teacher."

I felt in on a secret that I knew might shock or confuse the younger kids.

I was curious about whether students recalled our formal discussions about gay topics and, if so, how they experienced these discussions at the time. While these discussions loom large in my own memory as a scary time requiring weeks of preparation and being fraught with various risks, few students actually recalled the discussions, and those who did recalled few details. Instead, what stood out more clearly in some students' memories were conversations that occurred behind my back. Heather noted,

I do not recall any class discussions except behind Eric's back. There was a childish giddiness about the fact that Eric was openly gay and the normal remarks (sometimes inquisitive, sometimes hurtful) were shared amongst the kids in the class about what it was that gay meant and how it affected our comfort with him as our teacher (mostly the boys). Overall, there was an acceptance and appreciation for Eric's role in our lives.

Because I taught a mixed, sixth-, seventh-, and eighth-grade class, some of the respondents had experienced three different annual coming-out talks, as new cohorts of students entered our class. Stefanie was one of these students who heard more than one speech:

> I certainly remember the "annual coming out speech." I have fewer memories of the first time Eric told us he was gay, but more of the following two years when I sat patiently, but with a degree of blaseness, listening to him speak the same words to a new set of younger kids. I felt in on a secret that I knew might shock or confuse the younger kids. I felt infinitely more mature than the boys and girls who were listening for the first time and also critical of kids my age who made jokes about it.

One student recalled the coming-out speech as a time that was not comfortable for her. Hannah remembered,

> I remember when Eric told us he was gay. It was an intense and embarrassing meeting. I think I was mainly worried about what the younger kids in the class would think. Did they get it? Would they be able to deal with it?

Likewise, Laura recalled,

> The only thing I remember was the coming out day when we had a meeting and got to ask the questions. It was fun because it was about what every teenager is obsessed with. . . . I wish we could have had a heterosexual question and answer time too.

Nick was not in my class when I began teaching at the school and hence had access to information about my being gay before he had knowledge of me as his teacher. He wrote,

> I remember hearing before I started in Eric's class from a classmate that he was gay and was sometimes on TV being gay and we should expect him to tell us this. I was worried this would be uncomfortable for him and us and embarrassing. I remember him telling us he was gay but I remember I had been waiting for this for a while, so I don't think it was early fall. It was matter-of-fact. I don't remember any discussion.

During two of my years at the school, Cheryl, a teacher in our small teaching team, was out as a lesbian. Caleb wrote about a time when two of his three primary teachers came out to the class.

> I remember when Eric and Cheryl told the class they were gay, and I could feel how important it was (for them especially) to try to explain what that meant in a non-threatening way. I think they succeeded. I still saw them as regular people. I wasn't sure what the fuss was about.

One student did recall the context of my initial discussion about being gay and was able to cite the specific circumstances that brought about my coming out. Brian's recollections approximate my own of the first full-class discussion on these matters:

> What I remember was Eric calling a special meeting (or just dedicating a regular morning class meeting) to "coming out" officially to the class, for the specific reason that he was about to attend a march on Washington for gay rights. He wanted to address his reasons for doing so before the students saw him on TV, so that there would be no sudden, unexpected feelings of confusion or embarrassment or any distress whatsoever caused by finding out about Eric's sexuality in that manner.

Yet Brian's memories went beyond the actual catalyzing force for the conversation. He recalled some of the specific parts of my coming out talk:

> Although I don't remember the details, I know that he described what it was like to begin to figure out that he might be gay as a young teenager, that he'd had an early puberty and been very self-conscious—I think that's right, but don't remember much more about it. For the most part, it was very straightforward, and very sensitive to kids' feelings about it. He opened up the meeting to questions or concerns that kids might have about it. I don't remember what anyone said. I have the feeling that one kid—a boy—might have been kind of put off and asked why Eric thought it was necessary to tell us this. But I don't remember any more than that.

Nick recalled the context of my coming out to the class during another year but noted that student interest in the topic subsided quickly. He said,

> Eric was a brilliant educator and I think this has always stood out the most. The fact he was gay was really interesting to us for about a week. After that we were too busy with our own stuff to think about it much. I think the way he shared this with the class—bland, mostly because he was about to be on TV or something—was appropriate. In general I feel the teacher's sexuality shouldn't be a topic of conversation, any orientation. . . . I guess if a teacher is gay the students will eventually know and you can cut months of gossip with "Yes, I'm gay, would anyone like to talk about it?" Thirteen year olds won't.

I didn't think gayness could be transmitted.

Contrary to the arguments of some gay rights advocates that having a gay teacher will exert no influence at all on children, all of the former students felt altered by the experience. When asked "Do you think having an openly gay teacher affected you in any ways?" the respondents answered that this early experience served to "normalize" homosexuality, leave them open to relationships with other gay people, and reduce their own homophobia.

Two young men exemplify the "normalization" perspective. Max succinctly responded to this question by writing, "Having a gay teacher made me believe that there is nothing wrong with being gay." Nick shared a similar perspective: "Introduced to a *real live* gay person at this age I think it has always just seemed normal to me that some people you meet will be gay and some won't."

Hannah explained how this normalization of gay people served her during her high school years:

> It made me open to other gay people I met later (other gay teachers in high school, for example). When other people in high school were whispering and all wound up about teachers who they thought were gay, I hadn't really thought too much about it. It wasn't a big deal for me because I had already had a teacher who was gay. I felt like these other students were so immature.

Two other women discussed how this early work on gay issues affected their personal and professional relationships with other gay people in their lives. Laura, the development officer and business manager, argued that having an openly gay teacher made her more able to forge meaningful friendships with gays and lesbians as she grew older:

> It made me not homophobic or even not the type of homophobia where Cambridge-liberals-who-see-having-a-gay-friend-as-a-status-symbol-type-of-homophobic. It more has affected family members, friends, and co-workers (close and acquaintances) who are gay because they have one less person being weird about their sexuality around them—me. That's important.
>
> It's like that butterfly effect theory. Through just me, Eric slightly helped a handful of strangers two decades later. I can just be friends with gay people (if they're nice). I don't need to go through a "training period." They don't need to explain themselves. That's a relief. I am a mini-vacation in the heterosexual world.

Laura insisted that having an openly gay teacher had helped her form stronger relationships with friends and family members who are gay:

> It has helped me *tremendously*. I wonder if I'd be able to have real and close relationships with some people who I cherish if not for this experience. It was harder to be gay twenty years ago. It's a lot easier for kids now, but there's a chance I could have been uncomfortable around gay men or women, and I'm glad I was always spared that.

Heather, the securities partnership tax practitioner and mother of two sons, was caught off guard when she received the survey but believed that her first child's care arrangements may have been influenced by the early experience of having a gay teacher:

> I never really thought about how having a gay teacher in the 8th grade affected me until I received this survey. In looking back on the years since Eric was my teacher, I have probably been much more accepting of people who were gay albeit not consciously. I put my newborn son in the care of a gay man for the first 1½ years of his life. Some people questioned that decision, but he received better care from that man than any day care center could have ever provided. I never once worried about any misconduct or about my son being gay because of the care provider he had. I don't know if that was partly due to the experience I had with Eric, or if it is totally unrelated, but it didn't hurt my ability to accept difference in people's lifestyle choices.

All respondents agreed that having an openly gay teacher at a young age had made them more open to gay people and to the full range of human diversity. Several students believed that their openness as adults was enhanced by this childhood experience. Hannah summed this perspective nicely: "I also think that I'm probably more open to other kinds of people in general as a result of having a middle-school teacher who was gay."

Likewise, Nick believed that his ability to get along with others was enhanced by this experience. This is particularly important for his work with Outward Bound, where a cooperative spirit is critical to the collaborative wilderness experience.

> I think it did help. I feel I have an easy time dealing with pretty much anyone. Their sexual identity doesn't make me uncomfortable. And I'm glad it doesn't—that's a lot of people to be uncomfortable around! . . . Schools should teach our children what exists in the world around them. This world has gay people in it. It has Black people too. And Chinese. And pianists. Honestly, we aren't in a position right now to be turning down any good teacher who is willing to do the job.

Two of the male respondents believed that their views about political activism and discrimination may have been affected by having a gay teacher. John described how his current political views may have been affected by his elementary and middle school experience:

> Yes, I think it has had a profound affect on how I view human relationships. If any two consenting adults love each other, I can't imagine discriminating against them because of it. Now Fayerweather was a very liberal school, as are my parents (especially on social issues) so I am pretty sure I would have felt this at some level, however, I don't think I would have felt it as strongly if I did not have a person to tie it back to.

Brian was raised by counterculture parents in the 1960s and 1970s; he believed he was most influenced by seeing a politicized gay man as his teacher:

> I'd had other gay teachers, but I suppose in Eric's case he offered an example of a gay man who seemed very responsible and active in politics, and I think it was this side of the experience that was remarkable. He did not seem to fit any stereotype any kid had about homosexuality. It was not the fact of Eric's being openly gay that was remarkable. He was a strong personality and an effective authority. That made him notable as a person, but that and his sexuality had no real bearing on one another.

When asked "Did you ever wonder if you were gay because you had a gay teacher?" all respondents answered "No." Several backed up this terse response with broader explanations. Caleb explained how his views about the cause of sexual orientation led him to feel that a teacher's homosexuality exerted no influence on his own sexual orientation:

> No, I didn't think that "gayness" could be transmitted. I was not interested in exploring my sexuality (in so far as wondering about orientation) in 6–8th grade. In high school I wondered if I would ever have a girlfriend and sometimes wondered if I was gay when I didn't, but I never linked that questioning to my gay teachers.

Yet several former students thought that this early experience influenced their understanding of sexuality in general. Laura suggested that, as a result of having an openly gay teacher, "I was more comfortable with my entire sexuality probably." She stated,

> It helped that my teacher was so lovable and warm (despite trying and failing to make me a good speller). Twelve-year olds are squeamish and easily embarrassed (at least I was). I also respected him. This is all-important because it all, coupled with his seeming security in his sexuality and self-respect, was a definite influence in my shaping opinion of the entire spectrum of sexuality.

John recalled a critical incident that happened when he was in his early teens. He was participating in a discussion about gay teachers for one of the many media pieces that focused on our class, and it forced him to consider his own sexual identity:

> There was one odd event when Eric was on another local TV talk show and my mother and I were in the audience, specifically because I was a former student of Eric's. At one point, the host asked me my sexual preference, which left me a bit of a bind because I wanted to help dispel the whole notion that gay teachers lead to gay students, but at that point did not feel comfortable announcing

my sexual preference on TV. I ended up announcing my sexual preference and
have seemed to survive anyway.

Nick did not share the belief of Laura and John that understanding their
own sexuality was in part influenced by having a gay teacher. Nick experienced his teacher's sexual orientation fully divorced from his own: "I guess I
didn't really connect that *gay* had to do with sexuality. If Eric was it, it certainly couldn't have anything to do with my sexual feelings (Since day #1:
strong and for women)."

THE MORAL DEVELOPMENT OF IMPRESSIONABLE YOUNGSTERS

The small size of this sample of former students clearly limits generalizabil-
ity, as does the preselected nature of the sample. Yet, because the research is
focused in a field in which we have very little data, an analysis of the findings offers suggestions and possibilities rather than firm conclusions. The
data suggest that young adolescents confronted with an openly gay teacher do
not necessarily experience intense concerns about the situation. In fact, more
than half of the former students responding to the survey indicated that, at the
time, their teacher's gay identity did not loom large in their young adolescent
consciousnesses. Several of the students who responded to the survey clearly
recalled feeling aware of a disparity between the intense controversy surrounding the issue of homosexuality and their lived experience with a gay
teacher. Comments from two of the students suggest that, although they understood that they had a teacher with a highly stigmatized identity, they did
not spend much time considering the nature of that identity and were not interested in grappling with issues related to a teacher's sex life.

There may be several implications of these findings. First, they suggest that
the issue of openly gay teachers may be more meaningful for adults than it is
for children. While parental concerns, teacher anxiety, and the swirl of public
debate over an openly gay or lesbian teacher may seem intense, the issue did
not preoccupy these former middle school students or take a great deal of
their attention. While they were aware that their teacher was gay throughout
their middle school years, none of the students responding to the survey experienced this as a defining part of their school experience. In fact, several
students insisted that there were more notable things about their relationship
with me than the fact that I am gay, such as my height and size (which may
have intimidated them) or my political activism (which may have supported
their own interests in social justice).

Second, whereas the central debate on gay teachers is frequently focused
on whether they influence a child's sexual development or serve to channel

children into a homosexual orientation, it may be more helpful to debate the influence of gay teachers on children's moral and political development. Gay teachers might not turn children gay—all of these respondents self-identify as heterosexual—but they might make children less homophobic and, ultimately, less xenophobic. While researchers have probed children's identity development for many years (Kohlberg 1981; Langford 1995; Schulman 1985), the past twenty years of research into children's moral development have failed to engage gay and lesbian issues or suggest ways in which students' broader values and sense of morality might be affected by having an openly gay teacher. This suggests that openly gay teachers might serve a central role in the moral development of their students. Rather than fear that exposure to gay or lesbian people will "turn" a student gay or result in the rechanneling of sexual identity, educators might consider openly gay teachers to be a valuable resource offering authentic experience with stigmatized identities and issues related to "passing" and invisibility, as well as a deep knowledge of ways in which we as a society limit and constrain citizenry in the United States. If public schools are intended to serve the nation's citizenry, then gay and lesbian people are an essential component of all schools.

Being gay has also possibly allowed me to enrich the experiences of my students in additional ways. While some might argue that being a member of a stigmatized minority makes an educator more empathetic to others who have traditionally faced discrimination, I am not comfortable making that assertion. There are plenty of gay educators who harbor bigotry toward other groups, and being a gay man does not, in and of itself, protect a teacher from being sexist. Instead, I believe that my political viewpoints and commitment to social justice—rather than my sexual identity—made me into an educator eager to inspire empathy and action on the part of my students.

Perhaps the primary way in which my being gay enriched my students' lives was that it provided an accessible example of a person who resisted dominant social norms and managed to survive. During the adolescent years, when many students experience feelings of isolation and uniqueness, a teacher who occupies a space beyond social norms might serve to mitigate feelings of peculiarity and social dissonance. If the teacher can step outside the narrow boxes into which diverse human beings are shoehorned, then so can the student.

The greatest hope that I have for all my students—middle school or preschool, college students or graduate students—is that they will critically examine their social worlds; construct identities, bodies, and lives that serve their ideals; and never be afraid of bursting out of their boxes.

3

Rethinking Antigay Harassment in Schools

When I began my work as a teacher in 1976, few teachers—and even fewer school districts—had confronted antigay harassment, taunts, and violence in a serious and meaningful manner. Not only was it common to hear words such as *dyke* and *fag* thrown around in high school hallways and elementary school playgrounds, but it was not uncommon to hear teachers and coaches themselves using antigay slurs. When teachers at Fayerweather Street School, the school at which I taught during the late 1970s and early 1980s, began working with their students on reducing antigay comments, they were among the first educators in the nation to take seriously this matter, and they broke new ground in facing the daunting issues that accompany such efforts.

Over the past two and a half decades, educators in the United States have worked energetically to put into place the beginnings of institutional responses to homophobic harassment and violence in schools (Harbeck 1992; Jennings 1994a; Marshall, Kaplan, and Greenman 1995; Unks 1995a). Our efforts at the school site have primarily focused in four key areas: antihomophobia education; support groups structured on a gay–straight alliance model; the acquisition of gay-positive books, videos, and other materials by school libraries; and the development of "role models" for queer youth in the form of openly lesbian, gay, bisexual, and transgendered (LGBT) educators. Although significant progress has been made in all four areas (Walling 1996; Woog 1995), to many of us, it seems as if the level of persecution of LGBT and gender-nonconforming students has intensified with our efforts. How might this be possible?

This chapter grapples with issues that have often gone unaddressed as we have put into place what I have come to regard as the first stage of our efforts to transform American schools: Have specific societal shifts accompanied our two decades' worth of work and caused so-called dyke-baiting and fag-baiting to assume an increasingly central role in contemporary youth cultures? In what ways have the cultures of schools and the power dynamics embedded in teacher–student relations constrained our efforts? How might our limited knowledge of youth cultures, with our uncritical conceptions of children and youth (including our understandings of self-proclaimed LGBT adolescents), influence the tactics we marshal in challenging homophobic assaults? How might they constrain our effectiveness?

This chapter suggests ways in which first-stage efforts might be supplemented, reconsidered, and reinvented to challenge inappropriate (even harmful) assumptions about queer youth and address the ways in which the cultures, constructs, and power relations of schools limit our effectiveness. Rather than assist "gay youth" solely by addressing the institutionalized homophobia of the American education system (hence addressing the "gay" side of "gay youth"), we might aim to confront the powerful ways in which ageism and contemporary constructs of childhood and adolescence (the "youth" side of "gay youth") undermine our ambitions and reduce our effectiveness. Such changes would transform our work in advocacy, education, and service provision and create a second stage of work on antigay harassment and violence in schools.

Influenced by recent work on bullying and sexual harassment in schools, as well as by sociological writings on historical constructions of childhood, this chapter draws understandings gained from these fields into dialogue with antihomophobia efforts and asks the reader to situate our work in the broader contexts of gender justice in schools and youth liberation. By doing so, it may be possible to understand better the vicissitudes of LGBT issues in classrooms and youth cultures and to resolve some of the paradoxes that undercut our strategies.

The conceptual work presented here suggests that progress on social justice issues may not adhere to narrow and linear models of change that are frequently used to characterize and interpret success or failure and thus create expectations for incremental progress (whether swift or plodding) toward the eradication of oppression (Alinsky 1971). Instead, as influenced by theorists in popular education (Horton and Freire 1990; Pharr 1996), I suggest that what is discussed as "advancement" is often situated within a particular cultural niche while contradictory and paradoxical shifts may be occurring in other social pockets involving closely related issues.

Adherence to the linear model has often allowed those working on issues affecting young LGBT people, first, to conceptualize our work narrowly, focusing on secondary schools and only recently considering elementary and early childhood education; and, second, to keep it separate from broader issues surrounding ageism, sexism, and male privilege in schools. Most of the research has focused on schools with primarily white populations and fails to ask how struggles surrounding LGBT issues might look different in schools based in communities of color. The linear model has also created a significant blind spot that may have broad ramifications: it has led us to ignore ways in which adult activism may be making LGBT and gender-nonconforming youth more vulnerable to countervailing forces than that felt before our efforts, ultimately leaving these adolescents more exposed rather than more safe.

WHY QUEER-BAITING? WHY NOW?

Spending time in the hallways of many schools has led some educators to believe antigay slurs are the chief insults employed by students (Unks 1995b). Such beliefs understandably call forth competing claims by other populations who feel minimized or invisibilized: communities of color may feel contemporary manifestations of racism have not been factored into these calculations; advocates for special needs students might argue that offhanded insults such as *stupid, retard,* and *dummy* are as prevalent and unaddressed as antigay slurs are; advocates for gender justice may feel diminished when witnessing in youth cultures the popularization of terms such as *bitch* and *ho, slut* and *cunt.* It makes little sense to attempt to create a hierarchy of youth culture slurs and their victims and to compete for being the most persecuted. Yet something related to the ways in which gay and lesbian issues are situated vis-à-vis children and youth *has* changed dramatically in the past twenty-five years.

A few years ago, a leader of the Christian Civic League spoke on a panel debating gay issues in schools for a large undergraduate lecture class I taught called Current Issues in Schools. This man spoke longingly of the time when schools will return to the ways they were in his younger years, the 1950s. This was a time, he claimed, "when you could walk through the hallways of a school and never hear the word 'faggot.'" He insisted, "Conduct like that would get a student's mouth washed out with soap!"

One of my students responded, "That's because the word 'homo' or 'sissy' was the popular term at the time. I'll bet those words were heard frequently in the school's hallways when teachers were not present." This exchange raised several points that I continue to ponder. Some have argued that the rise of a gay rights movement, with the accompanying public attention to gay and lesbian issues, has served to expose queer youth rather than protect them (Herdt and Boxer 1993). Before the 1990s, the nascent gay movement received little attention in the mainstream media: we decried the failure of the

New York Times and other mainstream publications to take seriously the issues facing our communities; we protested the stereotyped visions of gay men and lesbians that constituted the sum total of our population's infrequent appearance in movies; and we were accustomed to being absent from television series. The 1990s saw a virtual explosion of attention to things queer, including gays in the military, the Ellen moment, the Versace murder and hunt for Andrew Cunanan, Jerry Falwell's attack on the Teletubbies—to say nothing of dozens of queer sitcom characters, independent films with gay themes, and queer rock stars ranging from Melissa Etheridge to George Michael to Ani DiFranco. With the ascension of MTV and the Internet, young people experience repeated interaction with discourses surrounding gay issues . . . whether they like it or not. This has only escalated in the new century.

Is it possible that shifts in the social position of things gay may trigger effects in young people to counter what we would intuitively expect? Have we been misreading some of the shifts in discourse that have been occurring? Have we been seeing only the effects on adult social worlds and not noticing the effects on youth cultures?

RAMIFICATIONS OF THE TRANSFORMATION OF CULTURAL KNOWLEDGE

While LGBT activists may celebrate these shifts in discourse, any transformation of cultural knowledge is complicated and fraught with risk. Few have considered the situated impact of contemporary discourses on homosexuality. Before the generation of these discourses, the thought may have rarely flitted through neighbors' minds that two women living together in a rural hamlet might be lesbians. Men entering the priesthood might not be assumed to be struggling with gay desires, and men and women unmarried at thirty-five might not be looked at with suspicion by relatives. In a short period, as it dawned on the public that same-sex-loving people existed, homosexuality increasingly became the default category in which Americans placed many people whose relationships fell outside of a traditional, heterosexual marriage or whose enactments of gender did not adhere to contemporary norms of femininity and masculinity.

This leads me to wonder whether the short-term fallout of social-change efforts might create widely varying effects that are situated in specific cultures and locations—religious versus secular cultures, rural versus urban spaces, adult versus children's social worlds, mainstream white cultures versus communities of color. I believe that this social transformation has had effects within youth cultures that may be quite different from the effects on adult cultures and that few adults have considered or understand. Discourse may create more cultural space for some populations (i.e., openly gay urban adults) while creating less for others (i.e., LGBT and gender-nonconforming children and youth or rural LGBT adults). As children and teenagers increasingly come in contact with gay issues from a variety of sources—not only media-generated sources but also by knowing or learning about openly gay relatives, neighbors, teachers, and peers—gay activists seem to assume that there will be a steady increase in comfort with and support for gay issues.

I hope this is true, but I am no longer sure. While children in some situations may become more accepting, particularly where children are permitted to ask questions and receive answers that are neither highly charged nor judgmental, the literature suggests that most children today inhabit social worlds complicated by competing notions of gender and sexuality (Epstein 1998; Epstein et al. 1998b; Epstein and Johnson 1998; Mahony 1998; McRobbie 1978; Thorne 1993). Pieces of information about homosexuality or interactions involving gay issues are dropped into an already highly charged mix.

Much of the theoretical work and many of the programs created to challenge homophobia in schools seem to be developed with little consideration of this volatile mix. For example, discussion of homophobia in schools frequently fails to engage valuable insights from research into bullying and sexual harassment. In fact, bullying, sexual harassment, and homophobic violence have developed almost entirely as three distinct lines of inquiry that rarely have been allowed opportunities for cross-fertilization. When I first attempted to publish a piece on bullies and sissies in an anthology on gay teenagers, the editor initially told me that such a topic was inappropriate for discussions of gay youth; after all, we should not imply that sissies are the same as gay male youth.

Much may be gained from bringing our work on antigay violence in schools into dialogue with the research and activism on sexual harassment and bullying in schools. Perhaps because definitions of *bullying, sexual harassment,* and *antigay harassment* remain contested (Beane 1999; Harachi, Catalano, and Hawkins 1999; Scarce 1997), few have attempted to untangle their distinctions. While some argue that these forms of "aggressive behavior" overlap (Beane 1999; Smith and Morita 1999), most theorists and researchers seem unaware of, and fail to reference, work in the other fields. Indeed, one could argue that these behaviors have been dispersed to distinct disciplines: bullying to social psychology, sexual harassment to women's studies, and antigay harassment to gay and lesbian studies. All three receive scant attention in U.S. educational research, evidence of the continuing challenges faced by feminists as they attempt to bring stronger analyses of gender and patriarchy into the field.

Research on bullying has advanced well beyond research into antigay harassment and may contribute much to our thinking in this area. School-based efforts to combat antigay harassment and violence typically employ a psychological approach to homophobia (Greene 1999) suggesting that a perpetrator's fear of homosexuals or homosexuality triggers aggressive and violent activity. The "problem" is situated *inside* a child, and programs intended to mitigate homophobia, interrupt antigay comments or activities, and "teach tolerance" are seen as the solution. Research, however, has shown that bullying unfolds in a peer context and that understanding the "social ecology of bullying" is critical to designing effective interventions (Atlas and Pepler 1998):

> Interventions to reduce bullying problems should not be limited to children who are at high risk for involvement in bullying problems, but should comprise a preventive agenda aimed at all students. A component of the intervention must be aimed at peers in several ways. First, schools must strive to increase children's sensitivity to victimized children and cultivate an ethos of peer support. . . . The second approach for intervention with peers involves lessons on the definition of bullying, providing strategies, and a language or script for intervening. Providing children with a language to stop bullying empowers children to use their voices and to take action against bullying. (95)

Indeed, entire books and handbooks for teachers have been published that offer comprehensive programs to root out bullying in schools (Glover, Cartwright, and Gleeson 1998; Sharp and Smith 1994; Stein 1996). Research on bullying has also demonstrated that the activity usually occurs away from teachers (Craig and Pepler 1997); hence, programs that rely on teacher intervention or hierarchical forms of authority may be ineffective. Qualitative studies of children's playground activities have shown that while girls and boys seem to be equally complicit in bullying, the two sexes utilize distinct bullying tactics (Atlas and Pepler 1998; Craig and Pepler 1997). Similarly, the literature on sexual harassment in schools offers similar insights into the ways in which peers, rather than teachers or parents, may be the most important line of resistance to such practices (Brandenburg 1997; Donahue 1998; Larkin 1994; Shoop 1994; Stein and Cappello 1999).

Indeed, bullying, sexual harassment, and antigay harassment may be alternative, age-appropriate manifestations of the same aggressive, power-based, gendered dynamic. Some studies have shown that bullying occurs in elementary and middle schools, then declines rapidly (Harachi, Catalano, and Hawkins 1999), whereas sexual harassment and antigay harassment are behaviors that seem to predominate during high school (Larkin 1994; Safe Schools Coalition of Washington 1999). When one considers the homosocial organization of children's lives and the transformations involving interactions with the other sex that occur during adolescence, an interesting possibility arises. Bullying may morph into sexual and antigay harassment as a result of maturational processes and rituals, the transformation of children's bodies, and the diversification of peer networks during middle and high school.

People researching antigay harassment or developing school-based programs to support LGBT and gender-nonconforming children and youth might learn a great deal from this literature. The limited ways in which we consider antigay behaviors in schools might contribute to our bafflement over the limited effectiveness of our efforts. Indeed, another lesson to be taken from programs to combat bullying and sexual harassment in schools is that even ambitious interventions fail to alleviate the problem quickly or dramatically (Donahue 1998; Pepler et al. 1994). Perhaps more radical approaches are needed, with a more dramatic transformation in the organization and culture of schooling.

With the limited research and analysis that has been allowed to occur on antigay harassment and violence in schools, we might lack a foundation of knowledge needed to quantify and make sense of contemporary trends. It is conceivable that while contemporary gay activism in the United States could be reducing antigay oppression in adult worlds, it could also be leading to a simultaneous increase in antigay oppression in children's worlds.

Understanding the situated nature of cultural impact seems critical here. Although it might seem easy to argue that taking discussion of homosexuality into the public sphere changes adult public opinion on gay rights matters (Yang 1997), youth cultures' relationships to gay and lesbian issues are likely to be more complicated than many adults imagine and may start to explain any escalation of queer-baiting and antigay violence among children and youth. At least three accompanying and countervailing effects may be currently occurring within youth cultures.

First, given the silencing surrounding discussion of homosexuality and sexuality in general it may be difficult for many children to make sense of concepts such as sexual orientation or sexual identity, which are now featured regularly in discourses to which they have access. For children, being gay is not easily equated with familiar identity categories, such as *black* or *female* or *Jewish*, categories of comparison frequently utilized in gay-inclusion educational workshops in schools. An eight-year-old boy may be confident he is male or black or Jewish because he can be provided with tangible evidence (penis, skin color, religious practices). Yet he is likely to be unsure about what *sexual identity* really means or what his own sexual identity is or will be. The injection of categories of identity into the social worlds of children—which, for most people, emerge more clearly during adolescent and adult development stages—requires them to make sense of something that does not easily connect with the ways they organize their other identities. This is likely to produce confusion and ambiguity, individual stressors and social anxieties that, for some, may trigger antigay sentiments and gay-baiting.

While parents might let children know they are male, black, or Jewish with some measure of confidence, what evidence is there that a six-year-old boy is heterosexual? Consider that specific notions and biases about the homosexual are culturally transmitted to children—for example, that gay men cross-dress; prefer to partner with other males; and are artistic, creative, flamboyant sorts. During a time when boys may be engaging in play activities involving cross-dressing, bonding with boys, or being artistic, it may be difficult for a child to make sense of it all. Yet, increasingly, that is precisely what we compel them to do.

An example brings this point to light. How do we respond to a seven-year-old girl who asks "Am I gay?" During an era when many children are aware that there is a stigma around things gay, how does an adult response of "We won't know till you are older" sit with a child? The film *It's Elementary* includes a young boy who seems to be anxiously asking if he is gay because he showers with his parents. What kind of answer can an adult with integrity provide that fits comfortably into that boy's consciousness and into the ways in which the boy understands the identities he has already acquired?

Second, the missing discourse of sexuality within discussions of gay and lesbian issues intensifies this confusion for young people; silence surrounding sex leaves children in quite a different place than it leaves adults. By discussing gay and lesbian issues as issues of identity rather than sex or sexuality—the "it's not about sex" and "gays are just like straights except for the gender of their partners" arguments—educators avoid raising "inappropriate" issues. Yet adults are able to fill in the blanks in a way many children are not. For example, when sex and sexuality are airbrushed out of an understanding of lesbians, and when we tell children lesbians are simply women who prefer women over men, we introduce concepts that with the gendered organization of children's cultures (Thorne 1993) might suggest that most girls are lesbians.

If a stigmatized identity—homosexuality—is presented to children in ways that, from their perspectives and social worlds, suggest that they might be gay or lesbian, it should surprise no one that we see an increase in social practices in which children find ways to proclaim that they are not. If lesbians are women who organize their lives around other women, and if girl culture is organized around other girls, girls who do not want to be identified as lesbian must find a way to distinguish themselves, police their and others' identities, and place themselves within a position of heterosexuality, or "not-lesbian." The identification of a stigmatized other—the peer who is labeled the "lezzie"—

serves this function. Teasing, taunting, and assaulting the identified lezzie allows others to create identities as heterofemales during a time that precedes the social stage in which significant social and sexual activity with boys serves the same function.

Third, the infusion of things gay into children's spheres has occurred alongside an escalation of masculine anxiety in much of the West (Connell 1995; Epstein et al. 1998a; Thorne 1993). The women's liberation movement of the 1960s and 1970s identified patriarchal cultural assumptions and exposed powerful ways in which sexism permeated children's lives, privileging boys while limiting girls. By the 1980s, it was no longer possible for boys to simply be boys because of biology: patriarchal privilege increasingly had to be seized. As women increasingly have asserted their rights to education, athletics, and job opportunities, and as gays have refused to remain in the closet and have emerged onto the pages of children's books, movies, and television shows, traditional masculinities have increasingly needed to be buttressed and defended. Boys have been forced to earn this identification by engaging in activities that bestow masculinity on them and by enacting a range of culturally specific performances of manliness (Connell 1989, 1995; Salisbury and Jackson 1996). Whereas boys' relationships with girls and participation in sports have been primary sites for these performances of masculinity, boys' relationships with boys and the intensification of a ranking system (of boy/not-boy) may have become more central.

Put another way, once the hegemonic nature of heterosexuality and masculinity have been called into question, boys have to find ways to make it clear to their peers that they are boys and not girls or gays. The privileges of heteromasculinity, once taken for granted, have to be affirmed and protected. Boys will be boys only if they perform the work of so-called authentic boys. Otherwise, they may be sissies, girls, or gays. An increase in antigay and antilesbian slurs may be linked to an increased anxiety surrounding biologized heterosexuality and the constituting of femininity and masculinity in our culture.

These three features of the cultures and worldviews of children and youth—the difficulties children might have in making sense of identities based on sexual orientation; the ways in which desexualized, homosocial constructs of gay and lesbian people might threaten children's social organization patterns; and contemporary anxieties surrounding masculinity and male privilege—may have moved gay issues and the identified queer into a central and highly charged position. The situation may be further intensified by timing: the need for children to separate themselves from being identified as gay or lesbian and signal a heterogender identity has occurred during an era in which some slurs and forms of banter that had been accepted as part of school cultures are increasingly frowned on, though in no way eliminated.

IGNORANCE OF YOUTH CULTURES
AND CRITICAL CONSTRUCTIONS OF
CHILDHOOD SABOTAGES OUR BEST EFFORTS

I have participated in dozens of educator trainings focused on rooting out homophobia and heterosexism from schools over the past twenty-five years, yet it is only recently that I have grasped the limitations of this sort of work.

As an early, openly gay middle school teacher in Cambridge, Massachusetts, during the late 1970s and early 1980s, I felt privileged to be able to educate my students and their parents about gay and lesbian issues. My school took seriously its commitment to consciousness raising and public education around homophobia. When neighborhood parochial school students painted *FAGGOT* on our building, our school community engaged in probing discussion about antigay oppression. When local television stations wanted to interview children about having a gay teacher, the school opened its doors. One year, a lesbian teacher created a girls' singing group and led them through women's music classics such as "Sister Woman Sister." I walked through those years thinking that my students "got it," and I was proud that they conducted themselves as good-natured, politically correct early adolescents.

When I surveyed those same students, then mostly in their early thirties, about their memories of their experiences of having an openly gay teacher when they were children (see chapter 2; also, Rofes 1999), I was shocked—and initially disheartened—to learn that some of my students often made fun of my gayness behind my back, used antigay slurs with one another, and derided our political discussions. Of course, I should not have been surprised here, knowing what I know now about early adolescence and tensions between teachers and students. I am left understanding that, at the time, I needed to believe such behavior was not happening, to continue functioning despite the stress of managing my various identities during that era.

I am also left with a powerful lesson about youth cultures and teachers' sense of omnipotence. How often I have instructed educators to interrupt homophobic comments and confront antigay slurs, believing that this is the larger part of our battle. Yet as I have learned about the oppositional nature of youth cultures and their independence from adult supervision and dictates (Austin and Willard 1998a), I have grown to believe that the portions of children's lives that are under adult surveillance and influence are actually quite small. While I continue to believe it is important for educators to confront homophobia when it arises, my faith in the power of educators to use such strategies to effect broad-based changes in consciousness and behavior is now tempered by the knowledge that teacher power and influence are limited—sometimes severely. Until we understand and take seriously the social, economic, and political factors that drive youth cultures and until we respect that accompanying social practices, rituals, and identities emerge for reasons that make sense to the young people immersed in those cultures, we will continue to maintain an overblown sense of teacher authority and a set of oversized expectations for our work (Brake 1980; Calluori 1985). I am suggesting that rooting out antigay harassment from schools will require us to confront the disempowerment and power abuses we visit on children through the ways in which we have configured power through the institution of schooling.

Developing a critical awareness of the ways in which socially constructed understandings of "childhood," "youth," and "adolescence" become central to our strategies to combat homophobia might ultimately serve to strengthen our long-term efforts (Aries 1965; Cable 1972; Cleverley and Phillips 1986; Cote and Allahar 1996; Griffin 1993; James and Prout 1990; Kett 1977; Pollack 1983). This is one of my core arguments in this book. On the one hand, gay educators have successfully argued that our understanding of young children as innocent and ignorant feeds destructive and sometimes abusive power relationships between teachers and students (Silin 1995). The film *It's Elementary* exposes the limitations of our beliefs that children cannot comprehend gay and lesbian issues by featuring grammar school activities where children exhibit their rich storehouses of knowledge in this area. One kindergartner articulates homophobia as "narrow-mindedness," comparing it to people who refuse to taste new food. Clearly, there are cases in which gay activists understand that contemporary constructs of childhood are part of the apparatus that keep school-based heterosexism in place.

At the same time, some of the rhetoric and many of the strategies employed in work on behalf of queer youth in schools support conceptions of childhood and adolescence that may function to undermine broader emancipation and wellness goals. Rarely do educators or activists working on issues affecting LGBT youth understand youth cultures as "specific social-historical formations" (Austin and Willard 1998b, 2). A "save our children" attitude underlies much of contemporary work with queer youth in schools, replicating current school-based paradigms of adult–child, teacher–student, and parent–offspring relations. The patronizing and infantilizing that occurs in some school-based programs contrasts dramatically with queer youth programs situated in community centers or organized as autonomous nonprofit groups that have embraced stronger, peer-based empowerment models, albeit imperfectly.

Many of our school-based programs have embedded in them unexamined assumptions, such as the following: queer youth are, in some ways, possessions of queer adults, just as children commonly are seen as a possession of their parents; the deliverance of queer youth from danger or persecution will come from a source outside themselves; adults can effectively serve as the protectors of children and youth.

The next generation of work in schools might reconsider these assumptions and recast our efforts along more liberatory and democratic models. In this case, gay and lesbian liberation cannot occur in isolation; it will require the broader emancipation of children and youth.

MOVING INTO THE SECOND STAGE

In a just society that has rooted out ageism and liberated its children, young people have sovereignty over their bodies and lives and are not the possessions of any adult (Kitzinger 1990; Lansdown 1994; Youth Liberation of Ann Arbor 1972). Certainly, adults support children's development and offer resources and care, especially during the years before their full emancipation and entrance into employment. Contemporary U.S. constructions of children and youth have relied heavily on child development theory to naturalize, even geneticize, characteristics that are socially produced: children are innocent or nonsexual; teenagers feel they are invulnerable to risk; without proper adult role models, young people's development may be stunted; and so forth (Kitzinger 1990; Silin 1995). Societies that infantilize and affirm children's dependence on adult protection engage in processes of cultural production that, while attempting to protect and care, simultaneously contain and restrict. Discourses to which children have access speak in a unitary voice: you need protection; you cannot care for yourself; your parents (or another adult) will protect you. Despite the fact that a majority of the abuses visited on children arise from these same adult sources, we mindlessly undermine children by placing them in dependent relationships with parents, teachers, priests, and coaches.

I am not suggesting that adult educators or parents have no role to play in creating safer environments for queer youth. Instead, I am arguing that we might consciously and strategically reexamine our current work and, at the very least, supplement our efforts focused on adult intervention, adult-initiated education, and adult-supervised support groups with models of education and social change that are fully peer initiated and peer based. We might further support LGBT youth by utilizing tactics of empowerment, providing them with education concerning their rights and ways to work the legal system, as well as giving them a solid grounding in self-defense and martial arts.

Our current focus for working on antigay harassment in schools contains one overarching misguided assumption that reveals a delusional omnipotence contained in much adult-centered reasoning. Many educators imagine that children and youth spend the greater part of their time under the watchful eye of adults and hence can be monitored, controlled, and corrected by the suasion of adult authority. They believe that the teacher alone is the source of knowledge and that students are blank slates waiting to be written on or are empty vessels waiting to be filled (Freire 1980). They also imagine that, even when a teacher is not present, her or his influence over students remains primary.

However, there are significant portions of young people's everyday lives where no adult is present. Even when an adult is present, it is often the students' peers who have the greater influence on behavior. In many schools, these times when no adult is present might involve the walk to and from school, the changing of classes, the time at the lunch table, the trips to the bathroom, recreation activities, classroom time spent in small groups, and field trips. Indeed, peer culture is the primary site in which a range of identities is constituted for young people. As Austin and Willard (1998b) have written,

> Negotiations of identity and autonomy are carried out *within* the peer culture and its internal segmentations as well; young people bargain for relative statuses and identities within the wider peer culture. The peer group has become one of the major institutions of socialization during the twentieth century, and recent studies indicate that the influence of the peer group for some populations is perhaps greater than any other institution. (5–6)

Approaches to conflict among children and youth that are predicated on outside authorities or adult threats may be effective in keeping homophobic comments out of classroom discourse but proliferating in areas outside adult policing. Until we engage in a balanced reconceptualization of the roles of teachers and students and a reenvisioning of schools as sites of democratic participation by students, we are unlikely to see a diminution of various forms of aggressive behavior on the part of students.

Imagine how the impact of our work on antigay slurs and violence might be different if, drawing on lessons learned from bullying and sexual harassment, a school community employed tactics different from the hierarchical, top-down approach commonly advocated (i.e., the principal takes a no-tolerance approach to harassment; teachers interrupt and punish antigay slurs; students are inculcated in "tolerance" for "diversity"). Imagine if the problem— harassment of gender-nonconforming or LGBT youth (Rofes 1995b)—were turned over to a student body experienced at utilizing models of democratic and popular education as well as conflict resolution to address community disputes. Imagine if the harassment were scrutinized carefully and in the public sphere, rather than dealt with swiftly and quietly; if survivors of taunts or assaults were supported to not feel ashamed by their victimization but to publicly name what had been done to them and by whom; if bullies and abusers were confronted and asked to explain themselves in a public setting; if the students at large were to create plans focused on deterring such abuses and were supported to abandon the role of passive observer of assaults.

How many harassed queer youth actually know about restraining orders or how to take one out against their stalkers or repeat harassers? If all gender-nonconforming boys felt competent to defend themselves physically, would there be fewer beatings and other physical assaults? If resources were devoted to peer-developed trainings for students about antigay harassment (and bullying and sexual harassment), giving them the words to articulate what was happening around them, would we see less of it or more?

I have no easy answers to these questions. Yet I believe these are essential questions that we should be asking as we commit ourselves to a probing reexamination of school-based efforts to support LGBT and gender-nonconforming children. If the first stage of our work in schools focused narrowly on educating and transforming understandings of LGBT issues while simultaneously reifying understandings of children and youth, we should not be surprised at our uneven success.

Our work's second stage must be broader and ultimately more ambitious. We must critically examine and transform the social and cultural position of homosexuality and childhood. Only then will it be possible to achieve deep and meaningful gender justice in our schools.

4

Innocence, Perversion, and Heather's Two Mommies

I have long been fascinated by the various ways that the organized LGBT community conceptualizes children and makes use of them in our political rhetoric, cultural products, and everyday lives. I recall queer responses to Anita Bryant's "Save Our Children" campaign, back in the 1970s, which insisted that the organized lesbian and gay movement was a threat to children. We would toss the slogan back at her and argue that it was *our* children—queer youth—who needed saving from the self-righteous hatred of Bryant's supporters. On a political level, it seemed as if we were having a custody dispute: whose possession were they, ours or Anita's? What did it mean that many of us left unquestioned foundational conceptions of children as put forward by the Right—that they were vulnerable and in need of protection? What did it mean that children were someone's possession, to be vied for, pulled at, and eventually owned as a kind of property until they were eighteen years old?

When early child custody disputes faced lesbian mothers and when our legal and political groups took up the issue of parenting rights, I watched with fascination as the movement struggled—or failed to struggle—with core conceptions of childhood. Certainly to win victories in courts of law for something as important as custody rights, it might have been unwise to challenge societal assumptions about childhood dependence and vulnerability and the various ways we understand parenting and "the good mother." At the same time, I knew lesbian friends who actively struggled with questions related to power in their relationships with their children, fiercely examining matters ranging from disciplinary practices to decisions about everything from food to bedtime to choice of schools. I greatly admired the fearless and searching assessment they regularly gave to their parenting practices, and I found myself wishing there were more queers—especially more gay men—who engaged in such examination.

The primary times where I witnessed gay men grapple with these questions involved debates about so-called intergenerational sex, or "man–boy love," and the North American Man–Boy Love Association (NAMBLA). While simply mentioning these matters in a book is enough to lead many people to discount one's thinking and question one's motives, these issues have historically provided a rare opportunity for gay men—and lesbians—to tangle with one another's perspectives on childhood and adolescence. While much derided, mocked, and undermined in the queer press and by other LGBT organizations, NAMBLA itself offers some of the most thoughtful critiques of childhood and adolescence and has questioned foundational assumptions about youth, power, and sexuality. Whether one agrees with their position on age-of-consent laws or man-youth liaisons, various NAMBLA-inspired debates have resulted in raising some important questions about age, sex, and power (Andriette 1983, 1992; "Community forum" 1992; NAMBLA Constitution and Position Papers, n.d.).

I have been fascinated by the gap between the ways many gay men narrate their own childhoods and how they talk about children from an adult vantage point. I have heard many men discuss their dawning sense of difference and emerging desires, insisting they were actively seeking encounters during their early teenage years. The stories they share are often about remarkably resourceful and persistent youth, eager to become empowered to have more autonomy and control over their lives and their bodies. Their testimony reveals an awareness of the limitations that popular understandings of childhood and adolescence have placed on their lives. At the same time, many of these men have failed to move this analysis of emergent sexuality into parallel and connected areas; they maintain a narrow focus on sex, without articulating the ways that economic, legal, and social statuses constrain young people.

All of this has spurred me to look closely and critically at the uses to which individual LGBT people and the queer movement have put children and youth. I do so because I believe that queers are in a unique position to challenge the organization of age into naturalized categories of childhood, adolescence, and adulthood. The experience of moving toward deviant sexual or gender identity while situated within families that embrace traditional notions of both suggests ways in which rethinking childhood, parenting, and the organization of family life might benefit future generations of queers. Our understanding more deeply the origins of childhood and homosexuality might assist us in these efforts.

PROBING CHILDHOOD INNOCENCE

Since the publication of Philippe Aries' *Centuries of Childhood* in 1965, a vast body of literature has probed cultural, historical, sociological, and anthropological conceptions of childhood. Scholars have examined theoretical models of childhood (Cleverley and Phillips 1986), literary images (Coveney 1976), sociological constructs (Jencks 1982), psychosocial development (Skolnick 1976; Woodhead 1990), and historical perspectives (Bakan 1976; DeMause 1974; Finkelstein 1985; Hendrick 1990; Kett 1977; Pollack 1983; Sommerville 1982); and have focused on tracing the development of child advocacy (Takanishi 1978), juvenile delinquency (Platt 1969), child rearing (Cable 1972), and children's rights (Holt 1975).

While sharing neither a universal conception of childhood nor an agreement concerning childhood's genesis and historical development, these works raise core questions concerning childhood as a social institution. Aries and his adherents argue that before the end of the Middle Ages in Europe, children were considered "small adults" and participated in a social and economic world with adults. After the age of seven, children commonly worked and lived away from their families and were integrated fully into the public sphere. The broad social interactions of community life exerted a greater influence on children than did the family, which had yet to be consolidated into a powerful, privatized apparatus of socialization and social control.

Between the Middle Ages and the seventeenth century, economic shifts were accompanied by dramatic changes in the child and the family:

> The child had won a place beside his parents to which he could not lay claim at a time when it was customary to entrust him to strangers. This return of children to the home was a great event: it gave the seventeenth-century family its principal characteristic, which distinguished it from the medieval family. The child became an indispensable element of everyday life, and his parents worried about his education, his career, and his future. (Aries 1965, 403)

Changes in childhood accelerated between the seventeenth and nineteenth centuries, linked to the rise of the modern, privatized family and its centering around the production, care, and socialization of children. As capitalism was extended and as it became the dominant form of economic and social organization, schooling was introduced and made universal and compulsory, hence providing the upper and middle classes with the mechanism to socialize the working class under the guise of preparing them for citizenship and employment (Katznelson and Weir 1985). During this period, childhood as a concept was solidified and invested with core attributes reflecting its essential state of being unformed or "innocent" (Takanishi 1978). Foucault's discussions (1977) of this historical period and his focus on "the means of correct training" and "the examination" are as much about the institutionalization of disciplinary powers as they are about the creation of the child as cultural product.

Over the last 150 years, conceptions of childhood have been consolidated and strengthened. Hendrick (1990) summarizes the recent developments:

> The new constructions stretched out towards three related and paralleling objectives. The first was uniformity and coherence uniting the urban and rural, embracing different social class experiences, and focusing on an allegedly natural state of childhood. Second, the font of this uniformity was to be the family, personified from the early nineteenth century by the bourgeois "domestic ideal" with its emphasis on order, respect, love, and clearly defined age and gender distinctions. . . . Third, from the end of the century a compulsory relationship between the family, the state, and public welfare services was legislated into practice. This built on the "domestic ideal" and, through psycho-medicine, reinforced the "natural" childhood in terms of education, socialization and dependency. (55–56)

Many contemporary theorists and practitioners argue that childhood is not primarily a social construction but a product of physiological and psychological factors that give rise to its essential characteristics and result in what we think of as the "needs" of children (Elkind 1981; Postman 1982; Woodhead 1990). Hence, the child is distinguished from the adult, while a web of disciplines emerges—child study, child psychology, child development, early child education, child and adolescent medicine—that encourages increasingly specialized and differentiated understandings of the child and that functions, depending on one's vision, to nurture and support or to isolate, study, categorize, and control.

Various conceptions of childhood have coexisted throughout this century. For instance, Hendrick (1990) discusses the "romantic child," "evangelical child," "factory child," "delinquent child," "schooled child," "psychomedical child," "welfare child," "psychological child," "family child," and "public child." As the conceptions have vied for preeminence, the child as innocent has been an ever-present yet shifting model. Aries traces its development to the end of the sixteenth century:

> Certain pedagogues, whose ideas were to carry weight and who would succeed in imposing their concepts and scruples on others, refused to allow children to be given indecent books any longer. The idea originated of providing expurgated editions of the classics for the use of children. This was a very important stage, which may be regarded as marking the beginning of respect for childhood. (109)

John Locke (1632–1714) has been cited as being crucial to popularizing a concept of childhood that sees the newborn arriving into the world unformed, unblemished, and pure (Cleverly and Phillips 1986). He describes the child's mind as white paper, an empty cabinet, a blank tablet, or *tabula rasa* (16). By the Victorian era, the vapidity of innocence becomes apparent:

> The innocent child is empty, all the more susceptible to influence. It is not a compliment to the child, then, to insist that deceit, for instance, is nothing more than "an acquired vice," that "children are not naturally deceitful." Not naturally deceitful does not suggest that they are naturally truthful, just that they are not naturally anything. (Kincaid 1992, 92)

Over the centuries, Locke's writings have been supported and extended by a range of philosophers, educators, psychiatrists, and social observers, and his views provide a foundation for contemporary perspectives that see children's knowledge, identities, and feelings as primarily created through the intervention of institutions of family, school, and religion. The supposed innocence of children has become "an ideology used to deny children access to knowledge and power" (Kitzinger 1990):

> The twin concepts of innocence and ignorance are vehicles for adult double standards: a child is ignorant if she doesn't know what adults want her to know. Those adults who champion "childhood" use innocence as an excuse to exclude children from "the adult world" and indeed, to isolate them from other children's experiences. In the name of innocence adults repress children's own expressions of sexuality, such as masturbation, deny children control over their own bodies, and seek to protect them from "corrupting influences." (161)

Similar social, cultural, and economic processes have created parallel constructions of "adolescence" and "teenagers" (Aries 1965; Bakan 1976; Kett 1977). Cindy Patton (1996) has probed the relationship between cultural constructions of the adolescent and "the discourse of innocence, sexuality, and HIV risk":

> The basic logic for separating the young deviant from the "normally abnormal" adolescent, and thereby determining who needs to know about safe sex, depended on the construction of normal adolescence as a passage from a precultural body (the innocent child), through a civilizing process (the adolescent with desires but without practices), to a sexually responsible adulthood (heterosexual, monogamous, married, procreative, white). (43)

A review of historical and contemporary conceptions of childhood presents a number of questions. Are children inherently different from adults, or is the distinction simply part of a strategy to allow power to accrue only to adults? Are the "care," "protection," and "education" we provide for children responding to inherent needs, or have these needs been created as part of a broad apparatus of social control? If childhood innocence is socially constructed, are current dominant views that present the child as asexual and without desire also socially constructed?

CONSTRUCTING THE HOMOSEXUAL

The creation of the "homosexual" as a distinct social type followed a path that parallels the invention of childhood in several ways: both terms required invention, determination of origins, and debate regarding definition. Jonathan Silin first drew my attention to these similarities in his book *Sex, Death, and the Education of Children: Our Passion for Ignorance in the Age of AIDS* (1995).

Before the nineteenth century, homosexual acts were subject to stigmatization and regulation, but individuals were not differentiated as "homosexual" or "heterosexual"—the concept of "the homosexual" did not exist (Katz 1990). European sexologists in the late nineteenth century classified individuals as types based on specific desires and behaviors, creating distinct categories such as "fetishist," "masochist," and "homosexual" (Krafft-Ebing, 1899; Moll 1931). Sexual discourse was already branded as dangerous, even by its champions. Krafft-Ebing was explicit in his concerns that the uninformed be shielded from discussion of erotic activity:

> The following pages are addressed to earnest investigators in the domain of natural science and jurisprudence. In order that unqualified persons should not become readers, the author saw himself compelled to choose a title understood only by the learned, and also, where possible, to express himself in *terminis technicis*. It seemed necessary also to give certain particularly revolting portions in Latin rather than in German. (v)

Connections between homosexuality and childhood were apparent in the late nineteenth century and are explicit in the work of Havelock Ellis (1942). As Ellis participated in the contemporary debate over causes of homosexuality— is it acquired or congenital?—his discussion reveals that both interpretations of "inversion" pointed toward childhood as fertile ground for the sprouting of homosexuality. The "acquired" camp believed that "sexual inversion is entirely explained by the influence of early association, or of suggestion" (302), whereas those who saw homosexuality as "congenital" obsessively searched early childhood for indicators of inversion. After reviewing existing theories, Ellis concluded that inversion "remains a congenital anomaly" that has "psychic concomitants," and he proceeded to "the consideration of the causes that excite the latent predisposition." To where did Ellis trace these causes? Again, attention was riveted on childhood, as Ellis fingered sex-segregated schooling and "the initiation of the young boy or girl by some older and more experienced person" for bringing homosexuality to the surface (322).

Linkages between homosexuality and childhood innocence were not invented by the contemporary radical Right in the United Sates. Shifting relationships between the homosexual and the child may be traced throughout the twentieth century in the work of sexologists and psychiatrists, of sociologists and urban anthropologists, of historians and social theorists; and such relationships can be analyzed in current formulations of the "gay brain" or the "gay gene" (Gallagher 1991; *Research Points* 1993). However, the period from 1860 to 1910 is rich with evidence of the development of a synergistic relationship between adult "perversion" and childhood innocence (Blumenfeld 1996). In England, the late Victorian period was a time when the homosexual was being defined (Katz 1983) and publicly reproduced through scandal (Weeks 1979). These years also saw the consolidation of childhood purity, the development of the child-saving movement (Platt 1969), and the construction of "female purity" (Walkowitz 1992). Jeffrey Weeks (1979) has identified connections between the social formations of childhood and homosexuality during this period:

> Changes in the late nineteenth century both encouraged and paralleled changes in attitudes towards homosexuality. Concepts of childhood are one such area. Childhood lengthened in the nineteenth century, and there was an increasing emphasis on the need to protect the innocence of children. Acts of Parliament sought to remove them from the contagious adult world of drink and crime, while state-sponsored voluntary organizations such as the Boy Scouts . . . were explicitly designed to distract or rechannel youthful sexual energies. Childhood sexuality became an important political issue. . . . The theme of the corruption of youth is constant, and the public-school controversy kept it on the boil. Working-class boys were involved in all the major scandals. (19–20)

James Kincaid (1992) believes that nineteenth-century sexologists' "offhand dissociation of pederasty from homosexuality" has been misconstrued and used to form the foundation of contemporary linkages (191). He cites "the ignorant, the unscrupulous, and the brutal" in the contemporary world who continue associating homosexuality and sex with children.

Jonathan Silin (1995) has made explicit the connections between the sexologists and "child-savers" during this period:

> The essentialist strategy central to the project of groundbreaking sexologists like Magnus Hirschfeld, Richard von Krafft-Ebing, and Karl Ulrichs was similar to that employed by nineteenth-century child savers. The former argued that homosexuality was not a sin of willfulness or indication of innate depravity, but rather a natural aberration to be accepted as part of the spectrum of human behavior; the latter rationalized their work by asserting essential, universal aspects of childhood that they undertook to protect. Unfortunately, these arguments from nature also confirmed both the homosexual and the child as special beings, members of discrete populations, who could be observed, classified, explained, and ultimately controlled. (189)

Silin searches for the "story of the pairing of the child and homosexual" in David Halperin's examination (1990) of the constitution of sexual meanings in the classical age and in Foucault's explication (1978) of the "petition to know" producing "new forms of knowledge" and transforming sex "from a matter of sensation and pleasure, law and taboo to a problem of truth that could be interrogated through science" (Silin 1995, 192):

> Like women, children were also in danger of succumbing to their own sexuality. Prone to premature indulgence, requiring constant observation by parents, teachers, and doctors, children were the enemy of the war launched against onanism. As with the project to control female sexuality, Foucault claims that the attempt to protect children from masturbation did more to sexualize the child's body than to deprive it of erotic expression. (193)

A number of Victorian physicians, mirroring societal concerns, attempted to "cure" children from what they considered "the disease of masturbation." The American physician and health food pioneer John Harvey Kellogg, for example, introduced a new line of foods at his sanitarium in Battle Creek, Michigan, designed to rid a child's body of "unhealthy impulses to masturbate." He called his new food "Kellogg's Breakfast Cereals" (Blumenfeld 1995b).

Silin synthesizes the nineteenth-century constructions of childhood and the homosexual and asserts:

> History links women, children, and homosexuals in the same nexus of unfulfilled desires. For it is the emergence of the mental health perspectives that announces the psychological needs of children and the unique abilities of women to fulfill them and at the same time defines the homosexual, threat to normal development. The homosexual, embodying everything that the child is not, allows us to see what the child is—innocent and without desire, a blank slate on which we may write at will. (194)

This linkage is neither the retrospective fantasy of historians nor part of some grand conspiracy that consciously plotted to situate the homosexual and the child on polar ends of an axis of innocence and corruption. Instead, within the grand sorting and categorizing of individuals that occurred in the service of rapidly expanding capitalism, types of individuals became imbued with a symbolism and social function that allowed for the privileging of segments of the population. Hence, social divisions were invented or deepened while a vast system of positionality—one based on superficial factors such as size, anatomy, and sex acts—was produced that affirmed the situating of white people over people of color, adults over children, males over females, and heterosexuals over homosexuals. The interconnections between varying categories became threads in a sweeping social fabric, to be pulled and tested in various directions during various periods yet to survive intact into our contemporary world.

JUXTAPOSING QUEERS AND CHILDREN

Gayle Rubin has written extensively about the historical function of sex panics (Rubin 1993). She defines "moral panics" as "the 'political moment' of sex, in which diffuse attitudes are channeled into political action and from there into social change" (25). Rubin cites several examples of moral panics, including the McCarthy era campaigns against homosexuals and the late 1970s "child pornography panic," and she explains that "conflicts over sexuality are often fought at oblique angles, aimed at phony targets, conducted with misplaced passions, and are highly, intensely symbolic."

The intensification of sex panic that occurred in the aftermath of World War II focused on homosexuals, and its linkage to incidents involving the sexual abuse of children has been documented by George Chauncey Jr. (1993), who writes, "As result of the press' preoccupation with the issue, the problem of sex crimes and 'sex deviation' became, to an astonishing extent, a staple of public discourse in the late 1940s and early 1950s" (232). During this period, a series of gruesome murders of children served as the spark to trigger mass anxiety surrounding the perils of postwar American life for women and children. Escalating reports of murders attributed to "sexual deviancy" appeared in the nation's newspapers and magazines and spurred "good" citizens to demand that the state intensify policing efforts.

Chauncey argues that postwar sex panic functioned to reinforce prewar social and sexual norms, which had become increasingly weakened during the war mobilization. Estelle Freedman (1989) also makes this argument and demonstrates that public concern surrounding the proliferation of lesbians and gay men in the public sphere merged with societal anxiety about the increasing freedom of children and youth in the intensification of postwar sex panic. Freedman writes,

> Although the preoccupation with "sexual perversion" appears in retrospect, bizarre and irrational, the incorporation of gay women and men into the demonology of the McCarthy era required little effort. According to right-wing ideologues, leftist teachers poisoned the minds of their students; lesbians and homosexuals corrupted the bodies of the young. (232)

This was reflected more recently in a Gallup poll that found that of those surveyed 20 percent believed that lesbians and gay men should not be employed as salespersons; 37 percent, not as military personnel; and 42 percent, not as doctors. When respondents considered employing gay people as elementary school teachers, the figure jumped to 60 percent (Gallup 1987).

Those working with children and youth bear the brunt of society's terror concerning the homosexual's influence on children. They frequently attribute reluctance to be openly gay to a range of sources that, when contextualized, appear legitimate. An essay by William G. Tierney and Robert A. Rhoads (1993) succinctly summarizes common feelings:

> Jack, an assistant professor, comments on the problems of being gay: "You feel the pain of oppression, of having mirrored back to you everyday that you're different and that there are people who want to hurt you, and deny you basic human rights." Other faculty express similar feelings: Diane, a tenured faculty member, remains closeted because she fears she will be ostracized. Jeri feels that "coming out" is too big of a risk: "I never wanted to see myself leading a double life, but if I were out my supervisor could do some real damage to my life." A similar concern is voiced by John: "I'm concerned with the way people view me. I'm worried [about] what people will think, worried they will say, 'God, this person's a faggot.'"

These concerns are commonly traced to societal homophobia and heterosexism. For example, a publication of the American College Personnel Association that focused on gay issues on campus presents a twenty-seven-page chapter that correlates homophobia with several factors, including an individual's gender role conformity and level of authoritarianism (Obear 1991). One overarching factor goes unstated that I believe lies at the root of homophobia—societal or internalized—and feeds a steady flow of anxiety and dread through the veins of homosexual men and, though to a lesser extent and in a different way, lesbians. A legacy of moral panic remains deeply lodged in the collective consciousness of queer adults.

CONTEMPORARY QUEER CONCEPTIONS OF CHILDHOOD

In attempting to counter arguments that homosexuals are perverted and pose a threat to children, the organized lesbian and gay community may choose a variety of strategies. In the early years of gay liberation, some advocated the liberation of children, viewing children and teenagers as a colonized population ready to break loose from the nuclear family:

> We want the abolition of the institution of the bourgeois nuclear family. . . . All oppressions originate within the nuclear family structure. Homosexuality is a threat to this family structure and therefore to capitalism. The mother is an instrument of reproduction and teaches the necessary values of capitalist society, i.e., racism, sexism, etc. from infancy on. The father physically enforces (upon the mother and children) the behavior necessary in a capitalist system: Intelligence and competitiveness in young boys and passivity in young girls. Further, it is every child's right to develop in a non-sexist, non-racist, non-possessive atmosphere which is the responsibility of all people, including gays, to create. (Third World Gay Revolution 1972)

Others addressed the issue of childhood sexuality directly:

> A note on exploitation of children: kids can take care of themselves, and are sexual beings way earlier than we'd like to admit. Those of us who began cruising in early adolescence know this, and we were doing the cruising, not being debauched by dirty old men. (Wittman 1972)

Current queer discussions of childhood, however, have a vastly different focus. A survey of literature, film, art, journalism, photography, and theater by lesbians and gay men reveals an absence of children in most areas, perhaps reflecting the separation of many queer lives from the lives of children. Discourse concerning children appears in several distinct areas: literary accounts of lesbian mothers and (less frequently) gay fathers, journalistic coverage of lesbian and gay teachers, records of public debate focused on NAMBLA and intergenerational sex, memoirs by lesbian and gay adults that reflect on their youth, and children's books designed for queer families. These bodies of discourse, while currently expanding and diversifying in political perspective, seem to share the general conception of children as does common mainstream American culture: children are objects or commodities to be protected, instructed, and controlled by adults. They provide women with identities as "mother" or "nurturer" (Lewin 1993) and men with opportunities to exert power, confront painful memories, or define themselves as "respectable" gay men.

Children's books offer one clear view into contemporary queer conceptions of childhood. For this chapter, I acquired and read almost a dozen books targeting children with gay and lesbian parents. They comprise the majority of books published by the only imprint focused specifically on gay families, Alyson Wonderland, a subsidiary of Alyson Publications. These books appear designed to fill a specific gap in the large field of children's literature and affirm to children with gay or lesbian parents that their families are as valuable as traditional families: having two mommies is okay; a dad who lives with another man is no big deal.

Hence, the books maintain an overriding focus on the family as the center of children's lives. The world of the child is centered on the family unit whether the book is explicitly focused on instructing children about

- different family configurations, as in *Two Moms, the Zark, and Me* (Valentine 1993) and *Families: A Coloring Book* (Willhoite 1991);
- facing childhood loneliness and boredom, as in *A Boy's Best Friend* (Alden 1992) and *The Daddy Machine* (Valentine 1992); or
- directly dealing with antigay prejudice, as in *How Would You Feel If Your Dad Was Gay?* (Heron and Maran 1991) and *Gloria Goes to Gay Pride* (Newman 1991b).

The books appear earnest and intent on illustrating that there are many valid kinds of family forms beyond the traditional, patriarchal nuclear family and accept without challenge the assumption that families and children are mutually centered on one another.

Within this worldview, a lesbian couple simply serves to replace a heterosexual couple as the source of knowledge and authority within the family unit. Children retain the characteristics they have been granted within mainstream American culture (cute, innocent, simple, and asexual), and the family unit in this body of literature escapes without being problematized. Despite the voluminous literature that unveils and critiques the underpinnings of the separation of queer lives from the lives of the hegemonic family—written from feminist and children's rights perspectives (Dizard and Gadlin 1990; Gordon 1988; Mintz and Kellogg 1988; Stacey 1991)—the authors of these children's books continue to paint a traditional, untroubled picture of family life and produce a body of work filled with traditional images of children.

The portrait of childhood painted by these books parallels mainstream views of childhood that have dominated Western discourse for the past two hundred years. School-age children turn to adults for assistance and knowledge in all things—transportation, designing party invitations, shopping, kite flying, inflating swim tubes, cooking, swimming, cleanup (see *A Beach Party with Alexis* [Johnson-Calvo 1991]. The objects, symbols, and activities juxtaposed with children include telling jokes and riddles, catching bugs, going on picnics and to the beach, tossing a baseball, making parents breakfast in bed, snuggling with stuffed animals and pets, and playing on swings. The range of feelings credited to children appears limited to two: happy and sad (Newman 1991a). Children are seen as simple people, free of complex and conflicting emotions. Two books tell the story of children leaving or becoming separated from their lesbian mothers in a crowd and finding hostility or dissatisfaction in the world at large before being rescued back into the warmth and safety of the family (see *Two Moms, the Zark, and Me* [Valentine 1993] and *The Entertainer* [Willhoite 1992]).

The child as innocent is captured succinctly in the description of Heather shortly after her birth in *Heather Has Two Mommies* (Newman 1989):

> Heather was a very tiny baby with big brown eyes and lots of brown curly hair. When she was very little mostly she ate a lot and slept a lot. Sometimes she smiled and sometimes she cried.

What does it mean that a line of children's books, one designed to fight homophobia and affirm the rights of lesbians and gay men to be with children, describes an infant in this way ("big brown eyes," "lots of brown curly hair," "sometimes she smiled and sometimes she cried")? Certainly, this is how many Americans see young children and how children's books have traditionally represented young children.

One could argue that the concepts and language need to be simple because the book is intended for young readers or will be read to children by an adult. Yet it is precisely this possibility—an adult reading to a child about the birth of a child who has two mothers—that brings into focus a series of questions about power and age. Do we want the children of lesbians to conform to prevailing notions of childhood in American culture? If these books present new parenting configurations juxtaposed with traditional concepts of childhood, whose interest do they ultimately represent? What assumptions about childhood—and about the ways we speak with children—would lead a lesbian author (or any author) to write the following:

> Mama Kate and Mama Jane both laugh and give Heather a great big hug. Heather gives each of her mommies two kisses. Mama Jane takes Heather's right hand and Mama Kate takes Heather's left hand and then Heather and Mama Kate and Mama Jane and Midnight and Gingersnap all go home. (Newman 1989)

These books, while successful at destabilizing traditional conceptions of gender and (to a far lesser extent) race, appear intent on consolidating the power of adults within a family unit and on rendering children as pure and dependent creatures. They present a queered construction of childhood not unlike the innocent child that achieved mass appeal during the Victorian period.

In critiquing antigay interventions into the education of children, Simon Watney (1991) has asserted,

> We may invert the usual question of what children supposedly want or need from education, and ask what it is that adults want or need of children in the name of "education." For it is in relation to theories of Childhood that the practices of adult power relations may be very productively analyzed. (398)

Watney's challenge might best be posed to lesbian and gay adults as we review conceptions of childhood in queer discourse. What is it that queer adults need of children? Do we see them as partners of equity in community life or as objects to manipulate in a broad political strategy? What does this say about our practices of power relations, and how does this affect the position of queers in the world?

It has become increasingly clear that such questions will appear "radical" and "outrageous" to a gay political movement whose center has moved sharply to the right in the 1980s and 1990s (Vaid 1995). Gay male writers increasingly embrace a traditional morality that naturalizes, biologizes, or geneticizes homosexuality and childhood (Bawer 1995; Sullivan 1995) and reflects a long-term assimilationist trajectory. As the sex panic is thus secured as a stable framework around which gay male identity is constructed, and as sex phobia and homophobia function to replicate the everyday social practices of denial, apology, and shaming that reify the cultural terror of the gay male imaginary, possibilities for liberatory shifts seem increasingly difficult to imagine.

THE MISSING DISCOURSE: CHILDREN'S LIBERATION

By reviewing the historical constructions of childhood and homosexuality, I have explored the roots of the linkage between childhood purity and impressionability and the supposed homosexual threat, and I argued that the two are conceptually linked as polar ends of the same conceptual axis.

A review of contemporary children's books for the children of lesbian and gay families illustrates current queer ideology on childhood and suggests that attempts to dislodge homosexuality as a disqualifying factor for parenthood are employing a strategy of reifying childhood innocence. Until childhood is freed from repressive constructs of innocence and ignorance and until the family as an institution is neither romanticized nor sentimentalized, society will seek, require, and even demand the services of the pervert.

The contradictory nature of the current strategy becomes apparent in a range of conflicts regarding gay, lesbian, bisexual, and transgender youth. In this case, gay activist rhetoric demands the right of children and youth to acknowledge and name their identities, even against the protests of their parents or teachers. Battles over school-based gay–straight alliances, antigay slurs, and cross-dressing students force advocates to embrace a vision of childhood and adolescence that is quite different from the innocence–ignorance model reproduced in the children's books. In these cases, advocates argue that children have rights to assembly, safety, and body integrity even if the adults in their lives (e.g., the family) disapprove. At the same time as they are championing children's liberation, advocates for queer youth market their programs to donors using the same "Save Our Children" rhetoric of Anita Bryant.

Is it possible to have it both ways—free the child and save the child? Is it an effective long-term political strategy to wrap ourselves in all-American images of parents, teachers, and children to retain custody or employment rights yet demand that queer children and youth have autonomous rights?

These questions emerge out of a political strategy that circulates around a large and gaping void. A missing discourse of children's liberation forces advocates to tip-toe to the brink of supporting a range of initiatives that hold the promise of radically altering the social position of young people but never diving in. Activist understandings conceivably could be rooted in knowledge of the powerful connections between the liberation of children and youth and the diminution of homophobia and other forms of antigay violence and bigotry.

Such an effort would aim to free children and youth from oppressive laws, regulations, and cultural constructions out of which emerge bizarre age-determined identities inextricably tied to innocence, helplessness, and economic and social dependence. We would eagerly respond to the visionary words of feminist Shulamith Firestone in *The Dialectic of Sex* (1970):

> Let's talk about what childhood is really like, and not what it is like in adult heads. It is clear that the myth of childhood happiness flourishes so wildly not because it satisfies the needs of children but because it satisfies the needs of adults. In a culture of alienated people, the belief that everyone has at least one good period in life free of care and drudgery dies hard. (107)

Imagine a generation of ten-year-olds able to navigate through the world as independent social agents. Imagine fourteen-year-olds able to operate economically independent from their parents. The failure in the United States to develop a popular discourse of children's liberation and the initial stages of a mass movement advocating children's liberation relegates the imagining of autonomous ten- or fourteen-year-olds to either the juridical realms of child abuse and neglect or science fiction and fantasy.

Yet accounts of childhood that have appeared over the past thirty-five years have uncovered a historical record indicating that such practices have been common in many cultures (Aries 1965; DeMause 1974; Hendrick 1990; Holt 1975; James and Prout 1990; Pollack 1983; Sommerville 1982). The movement for children's rights and liberation in the United States, while much discussed in the 1970s (Adams et al. 1971; Cuban 1971; Gross and Gross 1977; Youth Liberation of Ann Arbor 1972), has since been shunted aside to the realm of legal discourse, and child advocacy has displaced the liberation of the young as the dominant paradigm for youth work. While activity in support of children's rights has been building internationally during the past few years (Alderson 1994; Lansdown 1994; Newell 1989; Qvortrup 1993; Verhellen and Spiesschaert 1994), queer activists in the United States appear unaware and disinterested.

We need to develop new ways for queers to recollect, confront, and interpret the ways that homophobia and the colonization of childhood have worked together to wreak havoc on our early years. It is not enough to say that antigay, sexist, or racist bigotry makes the lives of children and youth into a hell on earth. The frequently quoted statistics on the disproportionate toll suicide takes on gay and lesbian youth (Herdt and Boxer 1993; Kourany 1987; Remafedi 1991) are as much an indictment of "adultism" as of homophobia. Testimonies of queer youth can be heard as narratives of heterosexism and homophobia, as well as ageism and the technologies that police childhood.

While radical changes in the social position of gay people and children and youth may appear to some to be remote during a time of the Right, it is apparent that gains made for homosexual adults at the expense of young people as a class end up increasing the misery of queer youth and perpetuating a cycle of oppression that maintains the status quo. Unless we gain an understanding of the ways in which power and knowledge circulate to produce vast multigenerational regimes of age-related oppression, queer youth will continue to be subjected to victimization as queers and as youth, and queer adults may remain one of the primary populations filling the requisite cultural role of pervert.

5

Queers, Educational Schools, and Sex Panic

In these days when queer studies conferences attract standing-room-only crowds and when academic publishers aggressively compete for lesbian and gay titles, it is easy for some to imagine that lesbian, gay, and bisexual issues have achieved a respected stature throughout the academy. Because some schools offer courses centered on queer topics, tenure queer faculty members, and strive to craft equitable personnel policies, many have come to believe that the stark silence of the 1960s, 1970s, and 1980s have been shattered. Not so.

Lesbian and gay issues stand at a critical crossroads in the educational arena. Efforts to create a scholarly sphere of lesbian and gay discourse may have been initiated but, with rare exception, have yet to be institutionalized. While significant achievements of the past decade cannot be denied, neither can educators pretend that the backlash against multiculturalism, affirmative action, and government funding for the arts and humanities is unrelated and poses no threat to queer issues in the academy. As the culture wars escalate during this period of entrenched conservatism, it seems critically important for activists and academics alike to provide vigilant oversight of all academic disciplines and all strata of schooling.

In an essay in *Radical Teacher*, Abelove, Ohmann, and Potter (1994) provide a concise summary of the achievements and limitations of queer studies in the academy. The authors note that much-touted advances "can easily seem more substantial than they are":

> Only a small fraction of U.S. colleges and universities offer courses in the field. Those few jobs that have been created in the field (and they are few indeed) are all, so far as we know, in English, American Studies, or Women's Studies departments. To the best of our knowledge, no department of history or any other

69

social science has advertised and filled a tenure-track position in lesbian/gay/queer studies at any U.S. college or university. (2)

Written in 1994, this quotation largely holds true today. In the field of education, only five universities have offered courses specifically focused on gay and lesbian issues (Harvard, Berkeley, University of San Diego, New York University, and Humboldt State University), and most teacher education programs include either brief, superficial content on gay issues in schools or remain silent on the topic.

This chapter examines the field of education's role in addressing lesbian, gay, and bisexual issues. I chose to focus my study narrowly on graduate schools of education because I believe they offer a specific and reliable window into contemporary theory and practice of education and because I conducted this research during my recent graduate school career. I begin by examining the mission of education schools and reviewing points of conflict concerning the purpose of schools of education. I then provide evidence of an array of contemporary gender and sex issues that confront educators in America. By considering these issues alongside the stated missions and objectives of schools of education, I suggest that if schools were to fulfill the essence of their missions, then considerable resources would be channeled into research, theory, and analysis of educational practice focused on queer issues in the educational arena.

Next I examine bulletins, course catalogues, and application materials from sixteen graduate schools of education that I obtained as I was going through the process of applying to education programs. I do this to assess the stated relationship between schools of education and lesbian and gay issues. In particular, I focus on faculty research interests, school policies, and descriptions of courses. I try to identify work on lesbian and gay issues and "read between the lines" to suggest areas where examination of queer issues might be occurring out of view. I then summarize my findings and draw some initial conclusions.

Next I appear as a native reporter recording and analyzing experiences from my own years as a graduate student in education who is interested in the study and research of lesbian and gay issues. I examine key incidents involving curriculum, personnel, and educational leadership and ruminate on my reactions to experiences related to queer identities, community formation, and intellectual exchange in schools of education. In particular, I examine my own conflicted reactions to issues of gender, sex, and sexuality as they relate to the culture and climate of schools of education.

Finally, I consider historical accounts of sex scandal and moral panics. By briefly reviewing the escalation of sex panics in the period following World War II, I suggest that they offer a way of conceptualizing a profound and often unstated conflict that faces lesbians and gay men whose lives intersect with children and youth. By drawing on narratives of lesbian and gay teachers—and on my own experiences in classrooms—I provide examples of the powerful ways that sexual shame, fear of public approbation and scandal, and tensions between identities constrict the lives of lesbian and gay educators. I conclude by insisting that the linkage of queers and children triggers real or imagined sex panic that functions to police many aspects of academic life—especially in the field of education, which is so closely linked to children. Until the sex panic is no longer firmly lodged in the mind of America whenever queers and children occupy the same spaces, schools of education may continue to abrogate a key portion of their stated missions and continue to cede leadership on lesbian and gay issues to other disciplines. This cries out for immediate correction.

The tone of this chapter is intended to be one of inquiry: I seek to assess the state of queer issues in the discipline of education and voice questions that emerge from this analysis. It is not my intent to point fingers or blame individuals, and the questions asked and issues identified are offered in a spirit of critique in which I often implicate my own actions. Because I consider the nexus of homosexuality and childhood to be a highly charged yet confusing conundrum, it is my greatest hope that this chapter sets in motion individual reflections, community discussion, and collective commitment to action.

THE MISSION OF SCHOOLS OF EDUCATION

In January 1995, the Holmes Group released the report "Tomorrow's Schools of Education," which challenges the leading education schools to rethink their purposes and redesign their programs to better serve the contemporary needs of American schools (Bradley 1995). As *Newsweek* reported,

> They issued a bluntly worded report in which they warned that unless America's schools of education institute real reforms, they should "surrender their franchise" in teacher training. ("Teaching teachers" 1995, 69)

The group comprises educational leaders, including more than eighty deans of research-focused education schools, and among their recommendations are to "make research, development, and demonstration of high-quality learning in real schools a primary mission," "correct loss of focus and program proliferation to focus on developing educators who work with young people," and "make education schools accountable to the profession and the public." The report places the needs of public schools in opposition to theoretical work on broad educational questions and insists that schools of education aggressively link research to practice and institute profound systemic reforms aimed at transforming the education of teachers in America.

A brief look at the missions of education schools provides examples of varied philosophical attempts to mediate these long-term tensions between theory and practice. The mission in general is often in the formal articulation of aims and objectives through which institutions reveal core values and articulate organizational vision. While some may consider mission statements as empty rhetoric intended to pacify varied stakeholders maintaining disparate interests, I believe they offer succinct ideological statements of organizational purpose that may be used to consider questions of institutional responsibility and accountability.

A letter from the dean of the University of Southern California's School of Education, appearing in the school's catalogue, presents a mission bridging research and practice:

> Despite our size and diversity, we pursue a common mission—we seek to transform educational institutions by helping achieve significant and fundamental educational improvements for all students through the efforts of educational institutions. . . . We seek to develop lines of research, programs of study and demonstration projects which hold promise for improving (not merely maintaining) the productivity of our educational institutions. (University of Southern California 1994–1995)

The dean goes on to stress the school's commitment to marginalized populations:

> Our work tends to place a non-exclusive emphasis on categories of children and adults who have historically not benefited as significantly from educational services as have other categories of children and adults.

The University of California at Berkeley's Graduate School of Education catalogue (1994–1995) provided a lengthy summary of the school's purpose, which states in part,

> Our concern is to advance educational scholarship and practice, with the goal of enhancing opportunities for diverse communities of learners. Our programs are designed to prepare teachers, administrators, scholars, and other professionals to become leaders in their respective educational settings. As individual scholars who form a community of complementary expertise and skills, we in Berkeley's Graduate School of Education are committed to developing the kinds of understandings and practices necessary for addressing the most challenging educational issues of our era. (7)

The catalogue then delineates a twofold mission:

> to engage in research and development of the highest quality at the very forefront of educational inquiry and invention, and to provide unexcelled leadership, training, and service for the education community.

These two schools' mission statements typify the public presentation of overarching objectives of the sixteen education school catalogues scrutinized. Schools of education appear to put forward visions of themselves as committed to cutting-edge research in the service of the lived reality resonating in America's schools. In statements mirroring Berkeley's aim to address "the most challenging educational issues of our era" and University of Southern California's interest in serving those "who have historically not benefited as significantly from educational services," many catalogues express a commitment to cutting-edge issues and underserved communities. The stated mission of the School of Education at the University of Massachusetts at Amherst (1994–1995) reflects these concerns and offers an explicit commitment to "social justice" and "diversity":

> The School of Education is dedicated to enhancing the practice of education through research that informs both the preparation of educational professionals and the development of public policy that affects education. Our approach is shaped by our fundamental commitment to social justice and diversity and by our belief in the essential importance of national and international perspectives as we approach the improvement of education. (83)

The graduate catalogue of Wheelock College in Boston (1994–1995) articulates the school's purpose and provides a statement of the kinds of diversity valued:

> The mission of Wheelock College, the improvement of the quality of life for children and their families inspires an honorable calling to the human service professions. This mission is carried out by providing a sound professional and socially responsible education for graduate students. . . . The Graduate School is committed to preparing professionals who can respond to the pressing social challenges of our decade. . . . Diversity in age, gender, sexual orientation, and in socioeconomic, racial, and ethnic backgrounds is essential to the success of these efforts.

The University of Chicago's Department of Education catalogue (1994–1995) includes a succinct mission summarized in the style of a sound bite: "to add to, preserve, and disseminate human knowledge." It goes on to express the school's commitment to assisting "policymakers and practitioners at all levels of education," who "turn to the Department for insight and guidance in the analysis of problems and for programs of professional preparation" (3).

As a class, schools of education typically appear to incorporate at least three key objectives in their missions:

1. to "help ensure the survival of the present and future generations with improvement in the quality of life" (University of Wisconsin at Madison 1993–1995, 2);

2. to be "responsive to the needs and realities of education" (Boston University 1994–1995, 5); and

3. to "serve all the people of the state and indeed the nation as a center for scholarship and creative endeavor" (University of North Carolina at Chapel Hill 1993–1994).

In sum, they represent the sector's threefold commitment to improve quality of life, respond to the contemporary needs of schools, and serve a broad and diverse population.

LESBIAN AND GAY ISSUES CONFRONTING AMERICAN EDUCATION

Even the casual American observer is aware that in the 1990s—the period in which these catalogues and school's missions were published—the field of education faced an array of challenges. Policy matters such as student assessment, school choice, and educational financing; curricular debates involving standards, canons, multiculturalism, and bilingualism; and operational issues such as school size and innovative forms of governance were just a few of the daunting items on the to-do lists of educational leaders. With public battles raging over the reform, restructuring, and redesign of school systems, queer issues in education may have appeared as simply another "special interest" demanding time, energy, and resources from exhausted organizations. A backlogged legacy of resentment carried by those who view multiculturalism as "political correctness" and affirmative action as "reverse discrimination" may explode at the mere mention of sexual identity as a compelling matter meriting attention at the highest level of leadership. Yet the missions of education schools suggest that the sector bears responsibility for addressing policy, curricular, administrative, and philosophical matters involving lesbians and gays.

A review of news items about schools during this period suggests that pressing issues involving sexuality and schooling were occupying increasing amounts of time on the agenda of school committees and school administrations and were appearing with greater frequency and visibility in classrooms throughout the nation. Faced with a range of thorny issues that few have acknowledged, studied, or analyzed, practitioners and researchers alike are left without rudimentary information that might "add to, and preserve, human knowledge" about lesbian and gay concerns. A recounting of key incidents, controversies, and policy questions that arose in the 1990s illustrates ways in which knowledge of and experience with queer issues are increasingly critical to effective educational theory and practice throughout the nation.

At the highest level of national policymaking during the Clinton years, political leaders came close to enacting legislation that would have taken punitive action against public schools for serving queer children and youth. In August 1994, as part of the reauthorization of the Elementary and Secondary School Act, which supplied public schools with $12.5 billion annually, the U.S. Senate voted 63–36 to withhold funding from schools that provide support to gay, lesbian, and bisexual students (Seelye 1994). A similar bill was approved in the House of Representatives (Griffin 1994). Constituent groups had to organize quickly and take public positions on this controversial legislation. Six national education organizations—including the National Education Association, the Parent Teacher Association, and the National School Boards Association—united in sending a letter to Congress that challenged the antigay amendments as a violation of local school control. While the antigay language was struck from the bill in negotiations between the House and Senate (Campbell 1994a), Speaker of the House Newt Gingrich labeled support and counseling programs for gay and lesbian youth "recruitment" (Diamond 1995, 5), and at least one congressman was not only amassing information to document public schools that "promote, encourage, or fund homosexuality" but also pressing for the prohibition of future funding (Hodgdon 1995b, 11).

Ironically, during the same period, the U.S. Department of Education internally wrestled with questions surrounding lesbian and gay participation in the workplace. The department revised its nondiscrimination statement to include the category of "sexual orientation." Secretary of Education Richard W. Riley told reporters, "We cannot tolerate discrimination in any form; we continue to pursue management practices that make equality of opportunity and respect for civil rights an integral part of all decisions that affect the workplace" (Walsh 1995b, 27). During the same time that Riley signed the revision, one journalist reported that the department had resisted recognizing the formation of an employee association of gay, lesbian, and bisexual staffers (Walsh 1995b) and that a department employee publicly challenged the sincerity of the secretary's assertions, insisting that "a means of addressing grievances filed under the new statement" had not been developed (Carnes 1995, 43).

Public officials and formal governmental bodies committed to addressing youth suicide have increasingly grappled with evidence implicating antigay and antilesbian cultural biases and documenting queer youth as a primary at-risk population, however problematic that designation might be. A much-cited report by the U.S. Department of Health and Human Service's Task Force on Youth Suicide (1989) recommends development of specific programs targeting gay and lesbian youth, acknowledging that "gay youth face rejection and abuse from family members and other youth and are often unwelcome in youth groups or recreational activities." After the document was attacked by conservatives during the first Bush administration, Secretary of Health and Human Services Louis W. Sullivan (1989) repudiated its findings, being sure to drive home his strong personal commitment to "traditional family values" and insisting that "the views expressed in the paper run contrary to that aim."

A few years later, six members of Congress sponsored a bill that would establish a National Commission on Gay and Lesbian Youth Suicide Prevention to address increasing public concern surrounding this issue (the bill failed, however; Campbell and Chibbaro 1995). U.S. Surgeon General Jocelyn Elders (shortly before her forced resignation) decried the "alarming rate" of gay teenage suicide, conceptualizing what had become a politicized issue as a "public health problem" ("U.S. Surgeon General" 1994, 22). As youth advocates, educators, and the Right engaged in increasingly strident debate on the role of public institutions in ameliorating gay youth suicide, the problem was brought home to the nation's community of activist gay teenagers by the suicide of seventeen-year-old E. J. Byington, a prominent queer youth activist in San Francisco (Hodgdon 1995a).

In addition to federal legislative assaults, gay, lesbian, and bisexual students faced an array of attacks on their right to full participation in schools throughout the nation. The student council of a Seattle-area high school passed a measure banning openly gay students from serving in school government ("High school council" 1993). A sixteen-year-old student at a Catholic high school near Toledo was given detention by a teacher for wearing a T-shirt saying "Boycott Homophobia" to the school's T-shirt day. The young man appealed his case to a school dean, who lifted the detention (Weiss 1995).

A young bisexual woman went public after dropping out of a Maryland high school, citing taunting and harassment from students after her sexual orientation was revealed following the school newspaper's publication of her book review about a gay male couple (Campbell 1994b). A Wisconsin school district was sued by a nineteen-year-old who insisted that the school was unresponsive to his complaints after repeated harassment and physical abuse from fellow students. The student and his parents claimed that the principal told them "boys will be boys" and indicated that the youth had been flaunting his sexuality ("News item" 1995a). They won a settlement of nearly $1 million. The Seattle–King County Public Health Department issued a report documenting seventeen incidents of harassment and violence against the state's gay and lesbian students in 1990, including students being beaten, spat on, stalked, rubbed against, and pursued. The report includes the rape of one young woman who was forcibly kissed by three girls who told her, "We don't want your kind, lesbian. Leave." The document indicates that three students in the state had been physically injured and that one had to be hospitalized as a result of an antigay attack (Van Bronkhorst 1994).

Academic studies have begun to appear that detail the conflicts facing queer students in a variety of settings, including schools. One study focused on lesbian students in Canadian high schools (Khayatt 1994) and spelled out the stark options that young lesbians perceive as being available:

a) concealing their sexuality and remaining invisible;
b) coming out publicly and putting up with harassment;
c) seeking a gay/lesbian community outside the school—an option not often possible for rural youth; and
d) leaving school. (59)

Another study focused on incidents of victimization owing to sexual orientation among members of organized social groups for lesbian, gay, and bisexual youth in fourteen cities. Researchers found the following types of victimization as occurring at least once and as reported by respondents: verbal insults (80 percent), threats of attack (44 percent), vandalism (23 percent), objects thrown at them (31 percent), chased or followed (30 percent), spat on (13 percent), assault (18 percent), assault with a weapon (9 percent), and sexual assault (22 percent) (Pilkington and D'Augelli n.d., 46). This same study found that 22 percent of male participants and 29 percent of female participants had been hurt by another student and that 7 percent of those surveyed had been hurt by a teacher because of their sexual orientation (19).

During the 1990s, teachers continued to come out in the nation's urban, suburban, and rural schools. Alta Kavanaugh, an English teacher at Alessandro High School in Hemet, California, came out as she was teaching a unit on prejudice (Gross 1994). In the conservative rural community in which she teaches, Kavanaugh discovered that "her fears about coming out were worse than the reality" (B8). Rodney Wilson, a twenty-eight-year-old teacher at Mehlville High School in suburban St. Louis, found support from students and parents but received a "gag order" memorandum from school officials focused on discussion of gay topics that fall outside the formal curriculum (Ruenzel 1994). During public hearings in Rhode Island on a statewide gay rights bill, gay elementary school teacher Marty Perry, Rhode Island's Teacher of the Year for 1994, told legislators, "I can legally be fired tomorrow for testifying before you tonight. . . . That's not right. We only ask that you judge us on our merits, not on our orientations" (Chibbaro 1995, 1). A variety of parallel issues have emerged in schools owing to increasing participation by openly lesbian and gay parents (Casper, Schultz, and Wickens 1992).

State policymakers during this period increasingly found themselves involved in educational matters involving lesbian and gay issues. In Mississippi, the state senate voted to withhold money from schools that taught "homosexual or bisexual behaviors," despite a state education official's insistence that no public schools do so ("Lesbians, gays" 1995). While a school board in Chappaqua, New York, unanimously passed a proposal prohibiting discrimination against gay students ("Bias policy" 1994), six districts in the state of Washington petitioned its board of education to remove a nondiscrimination clause that included "sexual orientation" in its language (Flint 1994).

Local school systems were the site of several major confrontations concerning questions about lesbian and gay issues in the curriculum, openly gay students or teachers, and library and classroom materials addressing gay issues. *Daddy's Roommate*, a picture book for children that depicts a child's gay father and his father's male partner, was at the top of the American Library Association's list of books that people attempted to ban in 1994 ("In 1994" 1995). *Heather Has Two Mommies* and *Scary Stories to Tell in the Dark*, two books that also include gay and lesbian content, also appeared on the list.

In Iowa, the Des Moines school system established a nondiscrimination policy that included the category "sexual orientation." It resulted in the superintendent's forming an advisory committee and charging it with recommending a plan for follow-up policy and curriculum changes to the school board (Freiberg 1995). After a school employee provided the director of a local antigay group with a copy of the draft curriculum proposal in December 1994, the antigay group promptly enlisted the services of a conservative talk-radio host who attacked the proposal daily. A subsequent rally drew three thousand people, and the following school board hearing attracted fifteen hundred participants. Within a month, the school board, acting on the superintendent's recommendation, killed the proposal and terminated the advisory committee. A school board member who had been elected to the position for a dozen years (and also the father of two students and a partner in the state's largest law firm), closed the board meeting with a speech acknowledging his gay identity. He subsequently received repeated death threats and began wearing a bulletproof vest to work (Von Uhl 1995).

In the early months of 1995, Fairfax County, Virginia, was the site of contentious debates about the inclusion of lessons on homosexuality in the district's high school sex education programs (Walsh 1995a). Five hundred people packed a school board meeting that heard, first, demands to remove the coordinator of the Family Life Education Program because of his alleged membership in a gay caucus of the National Education Association; and, second, accusations that the program's source book for instructors contained obscenities and pornography (Walsh 1995a, 1995c). At the meeting, school superintendent Robert Spillane stated his intent to remove the manual because it had been "so badly misinterpreted" (Walsh 1995d, 6). The school board voted 7–5 to retain the lessons on homosexuality but eliminated the teacher sourcebook.

In 1994, Massachusetts governor William Weld signed into law legislation protecting gay, lesbian, and bisexual youth from discrimination, and the state board of education approved a set of recommendations intended to ensure the safety of queer students in schools (Portner 1994). The governor initiated funding for the Massachusetts Safe Schools Program, which aimed to ensure that "gay and lesbian students feel safe and supported in their schools" ("Mission statement" 1993). By 1998, over half the state's school districts had created policies protecting youth from sexual orientation–based harassment, and over a third offered teachers training on issues facing lesbian and gay youth (Muther 1994).

In perhaps the most visible local controversy involving gay issues in the 1990s, the 443-page multicultural Children of the Rainbow curriculum was the focus of exhaustive and divisive debates in New York City. The document contained only limited references to lesbians and gays—namely, a reference to families with homosexual parents in a three-page section on family structure and three stories about lesbian and gay parents in the bibliography. These few citations ignited fierce political battles in one of the nation's centers of lesbian and gay community organizing (Glaser 1993). Battles over the curriculum proposal created deep divisions along racial and class lines (Lee, Murphy, and North 1994) and, in the opinion of the *New York Times*, resulted in the ouster of New York City schools chancellor Joseph Fernandez (Newman 1995).

Gay and lesbian issues were also asserted with increasing frequency in higher education in the 1990s and posed dilemmas for policymakers, administrators, and faculty members. A class at Kent State University, the Sociology of Gays and Lesbians, brought forth "strenuous objections from some students and state legislators," despite its popularity among many students (Cage 1994). The University of Idaho was the site of protest after a sign was left on the dorm room of a gay student that read, "We, the men of Upham Hall, do not care for faggots. In fact, get out" ("News item" 1995b, 10). At the University of New Mexico, gay and women's studies journals were defaced with swastikas and obscenities ("Vandals deface journals" 1994). Northeastern University's expansion of its affirmative action policy to support the hiring of lesbian and gay employees was the subject of an approving lead editorial in the *Boston Globe* ("Promoting diversity" 1994) but ignited debate among faculty and students on campus (Walsh 1994). Boards of trustees have debated continuing participation in Reserve Officers' Training Corps programs, given the tensions between school antidiscrimination commitments and the military's antigay policies (Crompton 1993).

Conservative students ignited public debate and legal action by pressing for the funding removal and banning of student gay organizations on a variety of campuses, including Yeshiva University, University of Minnesota, University of Arkansas, University of Texas at Austin, Indiana University at Bloomington, and Stephen F. Austin State University (Mangan 1995). The University of Notre Dame barred a lesbian and gay student group from continuing to hold meetings at the university's counseling center ("Note book" 1995). Students at Loyola College in Baltimore took out a full-page advertisement in the student newspaper calling for cancellation of a human sexuality seminar that included views of homosexuality different from traditional Catholic teaching ("Catholic school" 1995). A lesbian professor at Sacramento State University faced a $2.5 million sexual harassment lawsuit from a male student for discussions about lesbian sexuality in a sex education class, during which he claimed "the professor had made it clear she is a lesbian and tried to intimidate men in the classroom" (Wilson 1995, A18).

Studies of campus climates concerning students, faculty, and staff who are gay, lesbian, or bisexual indicate that "beliefs that gays are sick and unnatural and deserve to be punished are widely held—and acted out" (Tierney 1992, 44). One study of lesbian, gay, and bisexual students found that students felt unsafe in discussing sexual identity in classes and perceived a lack of support from faculty members or research on lesbian and gay issues (Yeskel 1985). Another college campus study delineated "hostile and unpleasant incidents" reported by students ranging from "the tearing down of posters for gay, lesbian, and bisexual events to being addressed with hostile remarks such as 'hey, faggot' or 'bash them back into the closet' " (Lopez and Chism 1993, 99). A survey of attitudes toward lesbian and gay men conducted at a large public research university found the majority of responses from faculty and staff (52 pecent) as well as from students (57 percent) to be "oppositional" or "hostile" (LaSalle 1992).

These are simply highlights of a panoply of issues and incidents that confronted education in America in the 1990s and continue to confront it today. From Rhode Island to Mississippi, Des Moines to Seattle, and Virginia to California, urban, rural, and suburban schools alike face daily a range of serious questions with tremendous legal, moral, and educational implications that did not present themselves so directly twenty years ago. Who is responsible for preparing teachers to respond to a fifteen-year-old lesbian who is harassed by peers? What kind of training assists a school committee facing a decision about whether *Gloria Goes to Gay Pride* belongs in the library? When a school district seeks research to determine potential impact of an openly gay teacher working with kindergartners or the legal rights of queer students to organize, to what body in the field of education can they turn?

SCHOOLS OF EDUCATION AND QUEER ISSUES

I now return to the catalogues of education schools, this time to assess the sector's leadership efforts on lesbian, gay, and bisexual issues. I use as my set of materials the catalogues I received while applying to graduate school in the 1993–1994 period. During this time, I obtained application materials and catalogues from sixteen graduate schools throughout the nation. While some schools were organized in a way that centralized all departmental materials into a single mailing, for other schools I requested and received distinct materials from specific divisions. For two schools, I had incomplete materials. The sixteen education schools that form the foundation of my study are listed in the appendix.

I reviewed each education school's documents twice. My first reading was intended to gain an overall impression of the way the materials represented the school's mission, philosophy, and divisional structure and to annotate specific references related to the school's work on lesbian, gay, and bisexual issues. My second review was a close, careful reading in which I highlighted faculty research interests, pertinent policy statements, and specific course listings that might include discussion of sexual orientation matters. I also noted specific omissions—for example, the lack of a nondiscrimination policy protecting lesbians, gay men, and bisexuals—and I annotated references that raised questions for me concerning things unstated or presented in a manner that suggested possible linkage with sexual orientation issues—namely, a professor with an interest in HIV issues or a research cluster focused on sex and gender.

After the second reading, I created a chart for each education school, including every reference I had noted. I then coded references in broad categories, including "classes," "faculty," "mission," "policies," and "silences." I attempted to articulate my general impression about the institutional involvement in queer issues, tracing my impression to specific items referenced in, or absent from, each package of materials. I then created a master chart of all sixteen material packages studied, and I developed a collective portrait of these institutions' stated involvement in the issues under study.

Faculty

Most of the materials I obtained from schools include information on faculty areas of expertise or research interests (thirteen of the sixteen schools). Some of these are superficial, including just a few words summarizing an individual's focus—for example, "curriculum/planning/evaluation" or "foreign language education"—but most are extensive enough for faculty to spell out areas of concentration; explain specific research interests; and list publications, awards, and positions in research centers. One school allows faculty members to include personal interests and family information, and several include photographs of each professor.

This area of investigation found little explicitly stated evidence of teaching, research, or publication in the area of lesbian, gay, and bisexual issues in education. The school that provides the most extensive space for profiles contains no direct references to these matters in any of the fifty-three faculty members featured. In all the schools studied, two faculty members mention work in these areas via their biographical sketches. Describing a book she coedited, one professor of educational organization, administration, and policy writes, "The volume calls up the voices of young people to speak as interpreters of culture—among them lesbian and gay students." A male associate professor working in developmental psychology is described as studying "barriers to safe-sex practices in Latino gay men." One school identifies a staff member in the list of adjunct/associate faculty with the title "Founder and Director, Program for Gay, Lesbian and Bisexual Concerns." Hence, three of the thirteen schools whose materials were studied provide indication of any faculty interest in lesbian, gay, and bisexual studies.

It was interesting to note that several faculty members who actually exerted leadership in research and publishing on these issues are identified in ways that do not include references to work on issues of sexual orientation. One leading teacher and researcher is recognized for work on "leadership issues of equity and multicultural education." The teacher edited a book that includes significant focus on sexual orientation, and although the book is referenced in the materials, its subject matter is not made explicit by the book's title. A professor who is a leader in utilizing cutting-edge queer theory is identified as interested in "postmodern theories," "critical social theory," and "cultural studies," but gay issues are not stated. Several professors are identified as maintaining interests in "gender issues" and "sexuality," but it is not clear whether this reflects active research interest and support for studies of lesbian, gay, and bisexual issues. The limited references in faculty descriptions to things queer contrasted with professors whose areas of interest and publications include references to the serious concerns of disabled students, women's lives, linguistic minorities, deaf children, at-risk youth, and students of color. The many references to research interest in "multicultural education" may or may not have reflected commitment to issues related to sexual identities.

Courses

All sixteen schools provided materials that contain listings of education classes, although I did not have complete course listings for two of the universities that provided separate packages of materials for distinct divisions. Among the schools studied, two courses specifically mention sexual orientation in the title: a clinical psychology course called Transference and Countertransference Arising from Differences in Age, Gender, Racial, Ethnic, and Sexual Orientation Backgrounds; and a module (half-semester class) entitled Staff and Curriculum Development for Antihomophobia Education. One university offers a class titled New Theories, New Pedagogues, which includes "an overview of prominent recent theoretical trends such as post-structuralism, feminism, ethnic and gay studies." Another school identifies "sexual orientation" as an area of inquiry in the course Anthropology and Education. These are the only additional education school classes located that use the words "gay," "lesbian," "bisexual," "homosexual," or "sexual orientation" in the catalogues' summary description of courses.

Appearing within several of the education schools are various classes that are neither exclusively focused on gay issues nor titled or described in ways that identify them as gay oriented. For example, the courses Perspectives on Human Sexuality, Psychology of Sexuality, Human Sexuality Education, and Sexuality and Disability appears in counseling and educational or school psychology divisions. Also being offered are courses such as Promoting Sexual Responsibility in the Era of AIDS, AIDS Education, and Talking with Children about HIV/AIDS. A variety of classes on child and adolescent development identify sexuality as an area of study. Classes such as Education in a Pluralistic Society; Democracy and Education; and Social Diversity, the Constitution, and Educational Reform might be appropriate forums for discussion of current policy matters related to gay issues but do not mention such topics in their catalogue descriptions. One university offers Critical Issues in Education and lists five possible topics, none of which involved sexual orientation.

All the schools offer classes that discuss multiculturalism in education. Such courses serve as possible sites for exploring issues of sexuality and sexual orientation related to American education. Yet titles and descriptions of these classes almost universally omit references to gay issues. Classes such as Seminar in Multicultural Counseling often define "multicultural" strictly in terms of race and ethnicity. Because descriptions and titles frequently spell out certain focuses, it is unclear whether inquiry into other focuses is encouraged or supported. One class is titled Problems in the History of American Education: Race, Gender, and Social Class. A course description for Diversity: Implications for Recruitment and Retention began as follows: "Students will explore aspects of cultural diversity and multiple oppressions (race, class and gender)." Teaching English in Diverse Social and Cultural Contexts is described in part as "a seminar examining how gender, class, race and ethnicity issues inform instructional goals." Sexual orientation largely went without mention.

Policies

Twelve of the sixteen education schools appear to maintain nondiscrimination policies on the basis of sexual orientation. Three of these are worth comment. One school articulates a sexual orientation nondiscrimination policy in the university's overall book *Courses, Degrees, and Information* (Stanford University 1994–1995a). It also features a "domestic partners" policy including same-sex couples. Yet the *School of Education Information Bulletin* for the same period, while including same-sex couples and heterosexual couples in "married couples" housing, states that the university

> has long had a tradition of admitting students without regard to sex, race, age, handicap, creed or national origin. Accordingly, the School of Education seeks to enroll a student body representing diverse backgrounds, viewpoints and interests, and is particularly interested in applications from members of underrepresented ethnic minorities. (30)

This may be a simple matter of oversight. Two additional schools, however, indicate a distinction between the constituting of sexual orientation nondiscrimination policy and other forms of protection. One catalogue states,

> In accordance with federal and state laws, no person . . . shall be subject to discrimination on the basis of age, religion or creed, color, disability, national origin, race, ethnicity, sex, marital or veteran status. Additionally, Governor Cuomo's Executive Order 28 and the University Board of Trustees policy prohibit discrimination on the basis of sexual orientation. (State University of New York at Buffalo 1993–1996, 56)

The inside cover of another catalogue states,

> Among the traditional factors which are generally "irrelevant" are race, sex, religion and national origin. It is the policy of [the university] that an individual's sexual orientation be treated in the same manner. The policy prohibiting discrimination on the basis of sexual orientation does not apply to the University's relationship with outside organizations, including the federal government, the military, ROTC, and private employers. (University of North Carolina at Chapel Hill n.d.)

Three schools do not include "sexual orientation" in stated nondiscrimination policies in their catalogues, and two of these institutions are located in cities that maintain municipal legislation banning discrimination on this basis.[1]

As indicated, several schools articulate special domestic partners policies that allow same-sex couples to share what was formerly "married student" housing.[2] One school features "sexual orientation" in a mission statement that includes discussion of diversity issues (Wheelock College 1994–1995). Another includes the following statement in the second paragraph of the description of its teacher education division:

> All programs require students to become knowledgeable about the development of children and youth; to value and support human diversity in terms of culture, ethnicity, race, gender, sexual orientation, and socioeconomic status. (Bank Street College 1994–1996, 63)

Finally, I was able to locate only one funding source targeting lesbian and gay academic pursuits. Teacher's College (1994–1995) lists the "James S. Scappaticcio Fellowship Fund in Clinical Psychology (1991)":

> Established by gift and subsequent bequest from James S. Scappaticcio (Ph.D. 85 M.S. 82) in hopes to further facilitate communication among students, both gay and not, and faculty, both gay and not, about sexuality in general and homosexuality in particular.
>
> Awards: annually up to two self-identified gay men or lesbians newly admitted to the doctoral program in clinical psychology. (31)

ARE EDUCATION SCHOOLS ABROGATING THEIR RESPONSIBILITY TOWARD LGBT ISSUES?

The limitations of a study of university catalogues and application materials are significant. Course listings may or may not reflect actual offerings that occur in education schools during a particular time frame. "Special topic" seminars may be offered that focus on the interests at hand, yet the courses may not appear in the catalogue, because they are offered irregularly. New faculty members pursuing lesbian and gay research interests may have been hired to work at education schools in the period after the faculty listings were produced. Some faculty members, as noted, are likely to pursue an active interest in queer studies in education, but the interest may not be reflected in the catalogue and course materials. Furthermore, schools that are not included in the study may be conducting significant research in this area and offering specific gay-focused courses to students.

Yet an analysis of the existing data, with these limitations in mind, is useful in gaining a general sense of the public representation of lesbian, gay, and bisexual issues within schools of education. For students interested in a program of graduate study specializing in queer issues and education, the schools examined here do not provide a rich, easy-to-identify pool of faculty members who share such interests. It is likely that such students, after reviewing application materials and catalogues, might come to believe that such research pursuits are unusual or unsanctioned by many of these institutions. Opportunities for mentorship, funded research, and collegial discourse on queer topics may seem to be limited in schools of education.

These impressions are reinforced after one considers the ways in which sexual orientation issues are silenced or only occasionally referenced in listings and descriptions of courses. Once again, potential students would not easily identify specific programs and courses that would directly focus on gay and lesbian issues in curriculum, administration, policy, and methods. Creating a graduate program with significant emphasis on this area would appear to require considerable independent work extending beyond formal course offerings. While some students might be able to pursue lesbian, gay, and bisexual interests in classes focused on sexuality, multiculturalism, and democratic education, such efforts seem to necessitate significant student initiative and independent work outside of course curricula.

A look at the annual meeting program for the 1995 American Educational Research Association supports a similar analysis. Interested researchers cannot easily identify significant programming that directly focuses on gay and lesbian issues. While "gay/lesbian studies" appears in the subject index of the program, only three of the conference sessions, out of a total of thirteen individual presentations, are focused specifically in this area. Furthermore, I was able to locate only an additional five individual presentations in other sessions that specified queer content. Hence, it appears that eighteen of the six thousand–plus presentations, or 0.3 percent of the conference's programming, was explicitly targeting lesbian and gay issues.

This analysis raises a range of questions concerning the role of education as a discipline and, particularly, educational schools in addressing the range of contemporary manifestations of lesbian and gay issues in American schools. I had knowledge of work being pursued by faculty members and students at some of the universities whose materials were a part of this study. As indicated, by a simple perusal of formal education school materials, the key educational leaders who have made pioneering contributions to this field of inquiry were not readily identifiable as maintaining such interests. It is difficult to assess whether faculty members self-censored, simply chose to omit their work on gay issues, or if the public relations staff and admissions officers who assembled these materials attempted to minimize "controversial" references.

Are we in a period when inquiry on queer issues is beginning to occur within schools of education but, through a variety of mechanisms, is isolated from the schools' formal, public documents? Do educators maintain resumes that privilege traditional or publicly sanctioned areas of inquiry over pursuits that might be considered risky, controversial, or forbidden within the discipline of education? What role do economic factors such as fellowships, job opportunities, tenure decisions, and research funding play in privatizing, silencing, or preventing education schools from fulfilling their missions' responsibilities toward the range of queer issues affecting contemporary theory and practice?

ONE GRADUATE STUDENT'S STORY

I reviewed these applications as an openly gay man with a primary interest in issues surrounding lesbian and gay issues in schools. I knew I could find experts in school reform, progressive education, and educational administration at most schools, but queer issues remained an open question. Hence, the application materials for graduate schools of education raised many questions for me. Was my area of interest appropriate to schools of education, or should I direct my attention instead to programs focused on sociology, law, social work, or public health? How would my resume and graduate school application be received if I included activities and publications that made my interest explicit? If I chose to pursue these studies in a school of education, which university would offer me an environment where these areas of intellectual exploration were valued and where I could find professors who pursued research interests related to lesbian and gay issues?

When I was applying, I sought advice from friends, teachers, and academic mentors familiar with schools of education. Some were professors; others were graduates of schools of education; and still others were practitioners or activist colleagues who already had faced similar questions. I received a range of responses. Most recommended that I discuss my interest and work on gay issues in education directly in the essay of my application. One colleague differed; he firmly warned me not to make gay issues central to either my application or my graduate program, citing concerns for my future employability in the field. No one I knew suggested specific programs that might include gay issues as a focus, and no one recommended professors with whom I could study in the geographic areas in which I was considering applying.

The Graduate School of Education at University of California at Berkeley offers a concentration in social and cultural studies, which at the time seemed to reflect my own interests, judging by the wording in its catalogue: "the study of education at its broadest" and "the study of sociocultural reproduction and transformation" (University of California at Berkeley 1994). The school's program description includes discussion of "a multicultural society divided by enormous inequalities" and emphasizes the socially and historically situated nature of learning. I looked through the list of faculty interests that included education and liberation, social theory, feminist methodology, educational issues in inner-city settings, and the construction of gender, race, and class. Of the program descriptions I had perused in catalogues of schools of education, this seemed to be the most suitable to my interests.

I decided to apply to this program to study the role that education plays in the creation and extension of social and economic inequities affecting gay, lesbian, and gender-nonconforming students. My application fully discussed my interests, publications, and work experience—all quite clear and quite queer. I was delighted when a professor contacted me several months after I applied to tell me of my acceptance. He wanted to be sure I knew that—while the division's approval of my application amid a competitive field reflected its strong support for my interest in gay and lesbian issues in education— expertise in this specific area of inquiry was not available within the division or, to his knowledge, within the education school. Division faculty certainly were available to mentor me in critical areas of interest, but the gay aspect of my work would need support outside the school of education. In this way, I would be pursuing studies as did all of the students in the division. Because the program values cross-discipline work, many students focus considerable energy in anthropology, ethnic studies, women's studies, sociology, public policy, geography, and history. Faculty and classes in those departments that emphasized lesbian and gay issues would form a large portion of the queer side of my graduate program.

Throughout my first semester in school, I wore a pink triangle pin on my backpack each day, and today I am not sure why that was so important to me. Initially, it may have been an easy way to resolve conflict about how, when, and to whom I should identify myself as gay. While a pink triangle is not recognized immediately by all as a signifier of gay or lesbian identity, in the back of my mind, the pin served as a check on myself that would not allow me to retreat into the closet, no matter how homophobic I found graduate school to be.

During my first month on campus, I was relieved to find a surprising openness to gay issues in my classes at the school of education. My statistics teacher informally presented a problem to the class that compared the number of personal ads in a local paper, focusing on "men seeking women,"

"women seeking men," "men seeking men," and "women seeking women." Another teacher introduced a lesson on the democratic tradition in education by discussing the bill proposed by Senator Jesse Helms that attempted to restrict teachers' discussion of gay issues in public schools. Because these matters were raised casually, comfortably integrating gay references into the broad work of the class—and because no one seemed to blink an eye (as might have occurred in the 1970s)—I felt increased safety and comfort within the school. I also noticed that the teachers who raised these matters were men who had already disclosed to classes their personal lives, including their wives and children. These did not seem to be closeted gay men launching a covert agenda in the classroom.

Because of these casual references and discussions in classes, it would be untrue to describe the school of education as dominated by a profound silence on gay issues. A class offered by a professor in my division focused on contemporary questions facing schools and included a week of discussion about lesbian and gay issues. One of the section leaders invited me to make a presentation to her class, as the course readings had already included a piece I had written about coming out to my students when I was teaching middle school in Massachusetts. AIDS seemed to be a common topic of discussion in the school, and this provided what seemed like coded language allowing gay and lesbian students to recognize one another amid classroom discourse.

I did not go out of my way to link up with a broader community of lesbian and gay graduate students outside the school of education, but when I met queer students or faculty, some of them provided a useful perspective on the recent history of queer issues at Berkeley, some perspectives captured in written accounts (Green and Ordover 1994; Klinger 1994). A faculty member in comparative literature who organized a queer reading group for graduate students sent me monthly announcements of meetings, but I never managed to attend. I did not find the time to attend the campus's social group for queer graduate students, most of whom I imagined were much younger than I was, beginning graduate school at age forty. Although I took a sociology class on "sexual diversity," which focused on lesbian and gay sexuality, identity, and community, I did not make efforts to connect with my fellow students, who were mostly undergraduates. I made my home in the school of education and found myself peacefully (if awkwardly) coexisting with the strange ways in which queer issues circulated within that environment.

Over the course of my first year, at least three things emerged that seemed odd to me. The first was that out of over thirty people on the school's tenured and tenure-track faculty, I was unable to find anyone who was either gay-identified or retained a significant academic interest in gay and lesbian issues. I asked faculty members and advanced students for leads but was consistently pointed toward professors outside the education school. I had no reason to suspect that individual professors were closeted or "discreet" except when I mused on the 10 percent figure attributed (incorrectly) to Kinsey's study and concluded statistically that several faculty members in the school simply must have been lesbian or gay. The lack of research focus in this area by people within the school apparently mirrors silences throughout the discipline.

The second oddity about education school involved the ways in which my fellow graduate students appeared to hold their identities as lesbians, gay men, or bisexuals. This is difficult to characterize, as it is based solely on informal encounters. Although there were a large number of queer graduate students, I met only a few during my years in graduate school who considered sexual orientation a key part of their lived identities at school. Fewer still expressed interest or concern with gay issues in the educational arena. One second-year student approached me in the campus grille one day and told me that he thought the pink triangle on my backpack was "so brave." When I pressed him to explain, he indicated that he was hesitant to be identified as gay because it might limit job opportunities. Another time, when I brought the topic of lesbian and gay youth into a discussion of access to educational opportunities in schools, a lesbian graduate student told me that she was unaware this was an issue in urban schools.

The third odd recognition involved ways in which I closeted myself in certain school-related environments. I observed a middle school classroom one afternoon, and the teacher asked if I would be willing to tell the children about my life and answer student questions. A panic attack immediately seized me: Would they ask if I were married? What would I say? What if they found out I was gay? I was shocked at how I attempted to wriggle out of the assignment and, when asked questions such as "What sports team do you like?" I didn't have the nerve to be honest and say, "None. I hate sports."

Another time, I found heterosexual colleagues assuming that my lover and I were monogamous and noted my tendency to accentuate my romantic relationship with him to feign a heteronormative queer identity. Once when classmates came over to our apartment for dinner, I found myself running about, nervously removing photographs, books, anything that would present an image of myself as a sexually active gay man. What was this about? One straight female friend, during a conversation over lunch, mentioned that she was "glad" that I had a "conventional" relationship and was not one of "those wild Castro gay guys." I found myself torn between challenging her assumptions and fitting in with her delusions. I felt shivers of panic run up and down my spine, mingle with hints of shame about my authentic sex life and my conflict about being direct with her. After sweating for several minutes and feeling like an imposter, I simply said nothing.

It is unclear to me whether my experience was typical or different from other lesbian and gay graduate students who attended this school of education. I had spoken with several who attended other education schools and noted similarities and differences in our experiences. Most of the time as a graduate student, I was grateful that my research interests were strongly supported by the faculty of my division, and I was motivated to find ways to take queer issues out of the margins of the discipline and make them a central focus of educational inquiry.

SEX PANIC IN THE CLASSROOM

In chapter 4, I cite Gayle Rubin defining moral panics as "the 'political moment' of sex, in which diffuse attitudes are channeled into political action and from there into social change" (25). What I call "schoolteacher sex panic" functions in agitated imaginations as a rapacious predator. It is constituted by powerfully constructed cultural messages that link filth, disgust, and shame to queer desires, bodies, and erotic imaginings. It places a rich backlog of constructions of the child as innocent, clean, vulnerable, and unknowing in a space with the wicked and infectious queer. Add to this haphazard recipe the power-charged erotics of the teacher as schoolmaster (parent, dominatrix, mommy/daddy, boss, all-knowing god), and what is created is an intensely symbolic and ritualized space penetrated by dread, terror, and unceasing anxiety.

Schoolteacher sex panic sits in the tidal pools of the psyche, unacknowledged and unattended, and drives an internalized system of self-surveillance and policing. This lurking sense of accusation, public outcry, and punitive sanctions is alive in what becomes a habitual, everyday practice of mediating co-constitutive identities as queers and schoolteachers. The messages delivered to us from the social worlds we occupy become lived reality in our everyday classroom lives, and they repeatedly regenerate themselves. The vast apparatus of moral panic creates the scaffolding on which we construct what we think are acceptable public representations of our social and sexual worlds. We live the double consciousness of the other, at times reading from distinct texts. The queer moving through our bodies as heretical gestures, inflections, signifiers, and hints of possibility is arrested, studied, and rechanneled into representations offering safe meanings that withstand social scrutiny.

Some of us may be more than conscious of our kinesics around children: we may be hyperaware of issues of physicality, spatial relations, and the geography of movement. Is any kind of touching worth the risk? What meanings will children and parents construe from my gait? Do I use my hands too much when speaking? May I be alone in my office with a fifth-grade boy?

We become conscious of the semiotics of clothing, commodities, and bodily appearance. How will this haircut affect classroom discipline? Are my pants too tight? Can I wear these sunglasses around school, or will they give me away? One friend who coaches women's basketball told me that she wonders each day whether anyone has noticed that she never wears "women's clothing."

We may find ourselves deconstructing our voices—scrutinizing tone, pitch, volume, accent, emphasis, timbre—and reconstructing elocution. Do we have to learn to be ventriloquists? Have dual identities create bifurcated intonations? Does schoolteacher sex panic make us masters of doublespeak, or are all queers, at base, bilingual?

Those of us who are at all open about gay identity in our work lives mediate a range of conflicting symbologies and meanings. What language do we use to articulate queer culture? In discussion, do we privilege those aspects of homosociality that correspond to values valorized by heteronormativity? Do we suburbanize our lives and appropriate "traditional family values"?

I ask these questions of lesbians and gay men whose lives include children because of what I perceive to be a recent escalation of rhetoric reifying notions of childhood and the family that have been long questioned by feminists, children's rights advocates, and critical theorists. A gay newspaper in Oklahoma is named *Tulsa Family News.* A line of books for children of lesbian and gay parents consistently presents conservative visions of childhood and family life (see Chapter 4; also Rofes 1998b). Also, an essay by gay writer Bruce Bawer (1995) has appeared in newspapers throughout the nation entitled "Family Values Key to Gay Rights." Today's battle over same-sex marriage will likely only sharpen this trend.

Judgments about gay and gender identity, "alternative lifestyles," and gay sex and desire lie at the core of society's inability to acknowledge the vast role that lesbians, gay men, and bisexuals of all races and classes have filled in raising America's children—as authors of children's books; as founders of children's service and social organizations; as child care workers and school teachers; as coaches of athletic teams and religious leaders; as youth advocates and policy makers; and as biological, foster, and adoptive parents. If it has been challenging to begin to confront antigay and antilesbian discrimination in schools under the rubric of "discrimination" and "homophobia," it is vastly more difficult to face the demonization of lesbian and gay sexuality that continues to serve as what Rubin calls "phony targets" for "misplaced passions."

Comments recorded in a research project (La Salle 1992) on campus attitudes toward gay issues by faculty, staff, and students provide examples of ways in which core components of the sex panic form the foundation of antigay attitudes, including disgust at queer sexuality, linkages to disease, criminality, the corruption of children, and violation of heterosexualized public spheres. Two responses are particularly telling:

> I'm fed up with kow-towing to sexual perverts! It's enough to have to coexist with people who are tearing down the traditional family structure. Don't cram them down my throat. If we extend special privileges to them, why not do the same for child molesters, etc.? They're perverts too!

> It is obvious that homosexuals are genetically inferior to heterosexuals, and therefore should be eliminated, before they contaminate the rest of the "STRAIGHT" world. If I were in a position of power I would implement this program to its fullest extent, to make the world a better place to live.

Many lesbian and gay teachers are familiar with the social awkwardness masking terror when some heterosexuals are forced to share "personal spaces" with queers. One Midwest lesbian academic has noted, "Some female colleagues even got visibly nervous around me in the bathroom" (Albrecht 1993). An essay discussing early childhood teachers who are male recounts one man's experience applying for a job (Skelton 1994):

> At the job interview, the chairman of governors said what would I do if a little girl was upset and crying. So I said I would put her on my knee and give her a cuddle. . . . The governor replied, "Oh no you couldn't do that, you would have to call the auxiliary." (90)

Narratives of lesbian and gay teachers offer examples of moral panic—internalized or external—and its effectiveness as a motivator of policing. A lesbian who was a junior high school science teacher in rural Maine provides one example that may encapsulate the core terror of every queer teacher:

> There were a couple of kids who were cheating on a test blatantly. . . . So I told them they would both get zeros and they needed to come in after school. . . . There had also been an incident on the playground . . . where somebody was talking about "one of those fags with a limp wrist," and that he was a real sicko. . . . I said people who are gay are not necessarily sick. . . . One of the girls went home and in the process of telling her mother that she had flunked the test for me, I think [she] must have softened that blow with telling this story about how I liked queer people so I obviously must be one. (Kissen 1993)

The girl's mother brought a complaint to the school's principal, but no punitive action occurred. A few years later, after the girl had left the community and then returned a year later, the teacher wrote her a welcome-back note.

The mother got that note . . . [and] decided that . . . I was trying to come on to her daughter. . . . She went straight to the superintendent . . . with this note saying that I was obviously trying to come on to her daughter and that I should be fired for that.

The superintendent initiated a series of letters to the teacher about how she "was never to be with students alone in [her] class at any time other than when [she] was teaching." Soon afterward, the teacher left her job, the profession, and the country. Moral panic takes its toll.

A college writing instructor provides an example (Luboff 1992) of the way in which sex panic operates internally. The man had not disclosed his sexual orientation to students and considered his public identity as "unlabeled" and "respectful of all people." A surprising confrontation calls forth the ever-present schoolteacher sex panic from the recesses of his mind:

A student recently offered to give me a lift in his car to the garage where my car was being tuned up. At one point during the ride, however, he became silent for a few minutes and then suddenly said, "I came out three weeks ago." My initial reaction was to remain silent, primarily because I had not expected to be made privy to such a revelation, especially not by someone who was stereotypically the idealized straight college student: good-looking, intelligent, bright-eyed, personable, and (most significant) usually surrounded by attentive female classmates. In addition, I was alone with a student and was concerned about what rumors, if any, might be started if he related this incident to his friends or to other faculty members.

Sex-based gossip, rumor, and public scandal are part of the apparatus of the sex panic. While this teacher feigns surprise as the primary factor triggering his silence, his own words suggest otherwise. Forbidden desires lurking in the subtext might ignite internal anxiety. On some level this teacher finds the student attractive. Confined in an enclosed space with a handsome student suddenly queered by intimate disclosure, schoolteacher sex panic bursts forth and freezes action.

In a paper entitled "The Sexualized Context of American Public High Schools," Donald Reed (1994) writes, "Although not generally recognized or acknowledged, the contemporary American high school presents itself as a highly sexualized organizational environment." Reed argues that "the school environment is exceedingly important in establishing the appropriate heterosexual identities of children" and is thus simultaneously "heterosexualized" and "anti-homosexualized. " He insightfully documents a variety of ways in which public humiliation, peer harassment, and institutional silencing function to preserve heteronormativity through schooling.

Desire in the classroom is the unspoken issue that must be grappled with if we are to undermine schoolteacher sex panic. Reed presents the school as a "heterosexualized" space, but I am arguing here for a remapping of the school as a sexualized space where a rich mix of erotics circulates and is repressed and denied in educational discourse. Desire, erotics, and sexuality are not acknowledged in classrooms and are not part of the formal curriculum of education schools. Instead, profound anxiety about desire is thwarted, deflected, and redirected into moral panic and then projected on stigmatized populations.

Michelle Fine (1988) has written about the "historic silencing within public schools of conversations about sexuality, contraception, and abortion, as well as the absence of a discourse of desire" (49). A parallel failure of schools of education to serve as spaces for extended conversation about desire, sexuality, and the politics of erotics has carved out huge disciplinary silences and led to vast abrogation of responsibility on the part of the field of education. A collective inability to develop a language that brings educational theory into the service of sexuality has allowed schools of education to make only a cameo appearance in the multidisciplinary theater in which discussions involving desire are staged (Rofes 1995a).

How does this occur? The ideological apparatus of the sex panic serves to buttress a scaffolding of homophobia and heterosexism that carefully and with deliberation construct an architecture of caution, omission, euphemism, and misrecognitions. Queers who work with children feel no choice but to compartmentalize lives, separate school selves from queer bodies, and allow the threat of economic retribution to vanquish authenticity. We find ways to live with ourselves and our decisions, and we often explain to ourselves that decisions are not decisions. What is the impact of compromise on our positions in our schools? What is its effect on our desires? When we work our way into the sticky webs of our disciplines and institutions and settle into comfortable uncomfortability, do we gain or lose motivation for collective action?

The silences of schools of education surrounding lesbian and gay issues constitute nothing less than the failure to lead. The field long ago relinquished sex education to psychologists, social workers, and sexologists. Over the past dozen years, it has contributed little to HIV prevention, ceding that contentious terrain to schools of public health. Currently it is in the process of yielding authority for queer studies to English departments and humanities centers. The Center for Lesbian and Gay Studies, at the City University of New York, lists in its *Directory of Lesbian and Gay Studies* 109 scholars in the field of English literature, 84 historians, and 64 anthropologists and sociologists. The number of individuals listed in the field of education is 13 (City University of New York 1994).

The responsibilities of schools of education in addressing lesbian, gay, and bisexual issues will not be discharged until educators become motivated to do their part in interrogating controversial and vexing questions amid an increasingly hostile environment. This is not a question of turf, as if disciplines could carve the universe into pieces of inquiry and discourse to distribute between branches of the academy. It is about whether we believe the field of education is constructed on values, paradigms, and visions of the world that have something to offer queer teenagers, lesbian teachers, or gay male professors beyond colonization or social control. Ultimately it is about whether educational leaders will find the courage to fulfill the mission and preserve the integrity of the discipline.

NOTES

1. The three schools are Vanderbilt University, Boston University, and the University of Southern California. The latter two schools are located in cities with formal nondiscrimination policies in effect.

2. Both Teachers College and Stanford include discussion in their catalogues of housing options for same-sex couples. In its application for residence halls, Teachers College includes an "affidavit of domestic partnership."

6

Bound and Gagged: Sexual Silences, Gender Conformity, and the Gay Male Teacher

In my current role as a university professor, I find myself curious about the relationship between two things I hold dear: my sex life and my life in classrooms.

It sometimes seems impossible for me to put these lives together or to understand that my identity as an educator is intertwined with my identity as a sexually active gay man. I spend most of my teacher life grading papers, counseling students, preparing and teaching classes, and observing in classrooms. I attend conferences focused on contemporary school reform initiatives, and I engage in rowdy debates focused on school choice, equity, and multicultural educational practices. I am immersed in ongoing study focused on historical constructions of childhood, urban youth identities, and the effects of charter schools on public education.

At the same time, I have an academic gay life that is partially focused on my historical research into gay men's sexual cultures of the 1970s, HIV prevention, and gay men's sexual health, and the experiences of lesbian and gay school teachers. Not only do I participate in academic and community-based conferences on these topics, but I also participate in ongoing work as a community organizer in lesbian, gay, bisexual, and transgender communities. I currently focus energy on organizing a national gay men's health movement. The week after I finished writing this chapter, I traveled to Washington, D.C., to meet with the leadership of major gay organizations to discuss how to address sexual scandals when they arise and how to combat the Right's intense sexualizing of lesbians and gay men.

Beyond my academic work, my everyday life reflects similar tensions; my body carries these contradictions. I may go from a three-hour block focused on preparing a new course to an exciting erotic assignation with a new friend.

My mix of identities and lives forces questions on me. Is it possible to be immersed in gay male cultures without picking up the habit of intense cruising in all social situations? How does my immersion in gay male cultures translate to my behavior at teacher conferences or my visits to local schools? Once, when I was having sex with a new partner, he asked me to "turn off the teacher rap" for a while. I had been using direct instruction—a formal pedagogical method I had used the week before with my credential students—in an entirely different, and perhaps inappropriate, arena.

Living in two very different places exacerbates this split. During most of the school year, I live half of each week outside a town called Blue Lake, deep in the redwoods of Humboldt County. My everyday life in the communities surrounding my university seems quite separate from gay culture, separate from gay and lesbian people. I am openly gay in my job, but because I have met very few gay men in Humboldt County, my gay identity there seems less sexual and more political or rhetorical. This is not a place where I regularly pick up strangers or spend a great deal of time socializing with other gay men. While there are informal social networks of men in this area, I mostly use my time in Humboldt County to focus on my work, not my libido or my social life.

My other home is in the heart of the Castro, the primary gay neighborhood in San Francisco, considered by many to be the primary gay city in the United States. My lover and I own a cottage just a few dozen yards from Eighteenth and Castro, the crossroads of the gay world. During the school year, I spend about half of each week in San Francisco. While there, I hang out at some of the local coffee shops with other gay male habitues. In the evening, I am likely to visit gay male bars in the South of Market neighborhood. During the days, I occasionally plan a "sex date" with a friend, or I find myself cruising and meeting a handsome man on the street and then going to his place or my place for a tumble.

My political views lead me to deeply probe the relationship between my life as a teacher and my life as a gay man. I have been active in gay liberation for more than twenty-five years and have worked in gay community centers, AIDS organizations, and the lesbian and gay media. While I have certainly engaged in mainstream gay rights work, my primary interests have focused on aspects of gay liberation that chart directions far afield from mainstream heteronormative cultures and social formations. I am not interested in a gay rights agenda that argues that lesbians and gay men are the same as heterosexuals and therefore deserving of equal rights. I am committed to a gay liberation agenda that argues that queer cultures have much to teach mainstream America about sex, gender, democratic social networks, and equitable relationships.

While the gay movement in the 1990s moved politically from the Left to the center (and some would say to the Right), I have maintained ongoing activism based in what some would characterize as the "Left fringe" of gay liberation. While I do some work on gay marriage, I am more interested in developing, exploring, and affirming patterns of kinship that are not based on a nuclear family structure or a traditional, "committed," gendered dyad. Gender-nonconforming men and women have been shunted aside by a gay rights movement hungry for "respectable" leaders who have mass appeal because they do not threaten the status quo; however, I am fixated on the social and cultural power emerging from troubling, subverting, and violating gender norms. During a time when AIDS has served as a convenient excuse for social critics to declare an end to a "failed" sexual revolution, I continue to immerse myself in communities that value and prioritize sex, and I organize my social and sexual practices in ways that can be described as "nonmonogamous," "promiscuous," or (drawing on Whitman's poems) profoundly "democratic" in spirit.

Each day when I wake up, at least two people move in me: the teacher and the lover. I do not view these two aspects of my life as contradictory or paradoxical, though I know others might. During most of my career in education I have juggled two public identities—the educator and the gay liberationist— and I have attempted to understand their intersections and explore the tensions that emerge from their simultaneity. For a long time I have suspected that some people with whom I work in schools and on educational policy matters would find problematic those aspects of the way I enact my sexual identity. I have also noticed that some colleagues in gay and lesbian movement work discount my work in schools or have no interest at all in my educational efforts.

At times, I feel deeply divided, ricocheting between extremes. I might check my answering machine at home in San Francisco on a Sunday afternoon, and there will be a student calling with questions about white racial formations or the purpose of public education in a democracy, questions for the following day's midterm examination. The next message might be from my lover, who is calling to inform me he will be late for dinner as he is meeting his boyfriend for a late-afternoon romp. I might do an Internet search under my name and turn up seemingly paradoxical listings: a selection of explicit sex writings from my latest book precedes a report from an education newspaper about my charter school research.

Although I may feel as though my life is split down the middle, intellectually I believe my work in education and gay liberation emerges from the same source: a commitment to creating sites that resist, undermine, and throw off institutionalized forms of oppression that have become endemic to life in the

United States. My interest in school reform is motivated by a desire to see urban schools become places that expand the critical consciousness of poor young people and that provide tools for social and political change. My interest in undermining gender as a normalizing and oppressive construct emerges from my awareness of the continuing power of patriarchy to limit the life chances of girls, women, and gender-nonconforming boys. Although sexual freedom is a problematic term, especially when bandied about in post-AIDS America, for me it offers insights into the transformative possibilities of pleasure in an advanced capitalist system that has succeeded in commodifying and gaining monopoly over most forms of leisure, play, and pleasure (Bronski 1998).

Ultimately, I believe my work as a teacher is about supporting students as they become agents of transgression and activists for social and political change. My mission as an educator is best captured by bell hooks in the introduction to her book *Teaching to Transgress: Education as the Practice of Freedom* (1994):

> The classroom remains the most radical space of possibility in the academy. . . .
> I add my voice to the collective call for renewal and rejuvenation in our teaching practices. . . . I celebrate teaching that enables transgressions—a movement against and beyond boundaries. It is that movement which makes education the practice of freedom. (12)

Yet I often feel an overwhelming hunger to learn from other educators who share similar values about how they construct their various identities and practices and how their work in schools and with children intersects with deeply held but often transgressive values. I am interested not only in teaching students to transgress but also in finding ways to continue to engage myself in transgressive activism and social practices during midlife years, when many previously radical friends have made compromises and embraced politically problematic social and economic practices. I hunger for a community of educators who live out our class, gender, race, and sex politics, not simply in our teaching or our academic publishing, but in our everyday lives.

I am most eager to learn from other gay male educators who may face similar barriers, fears, and points of controversy. Are there ways to situate ourselves in relationship to activities common to some contemporary gay cultures—such as cybersex, sex work, drag, sex in parks, or participation in leather subcultures—without denying our own interest or participation, feeling shame, or being ejected from our profession? Are the only alternatives available to gay male teachers to remain chastely single and perform asexuality; be blissfully wedded to a monogamous long-term spouse; or maintain strict boundaries between our sexual communities, practices, and identities and our teaching? Can we begin a conversation about the challenges facing male educators who do not perform traditional masculinities, a conversation that ironically has been initiated, not by gay male teachers or the groups that purport to represent us, but by the film *In and Out*? Or do we have to pretend that gay male educators as a class enact masculinity in only traditional ways and that none of us camp; lisp; utilize effeminate inflections, diction, or gestures; or cross our legs in class in the "wrong" way?

I do not deceive myself and pretend that I represent the majority of gay male teachers currently working with children in the United States. The liberationist project of the 1970s had long ago taken a backseat to assimilationist values in gay movement circles (Vaid 1995). Many men may share similar everyday stigmatized social practices and kinship formations—for example, sexual activity that is not limited to a single partner; gender performances that play with hypermasculinity, effeminacy, drag, and "butch–femme" dynamics; patterns of social relations that are centered on friendships and communities rather than on a dyad or nuclear family. But few maintain critical consciousness about these practices or place them in a politicized ideological framework. I want to talk with the ones who do.

My thinking on these matters has clearly been influenced by a privileged geography of pedagogy. All my teaching has occurred in the United States, a nation with its own paradoxical mix of sexual obsessions and sexual shames. My elementary and middle school assignments occurred in the Boston area, generally regarded as a bastion of liberalism, or at least open-mindedness. My college teaching began at the University of California–Berkeley, long a center of radical politics, even though it has become more conservative and a bit problematic around gay and lesbian issues in recent years (Klinger 1994). Whereas theorists have effectively made the case that learning is situated (Lave and Wenger 1991), rarely do educators acknowledge the situated nature of teaching or understand its implications for pedagogical practices. Yet a year's teaching at an elite college on the coast of Maine—an institution dominated by remnants of New England's conservative WASP traditions and cultures—has impressed on me the challenge of adapting my various identities, teaching styles, and educational objectives to an institution of higher education not known for its radicalism. While there, I found ways to maintain philosophical and pedagogical integrity, but the trade-offs, compromises, and risks were quite different from those of my Berkeley days. I now teach at Humboldt State University, which feels to me as though having the best of both previous worlds: the school is isolated and rural, yet the student body and faculty are among the most politically progressive in the nation.

I proceed in this chapter to look at representations of gay male schoolteachers in discourses produced by gay men. My objective is to illustrate how gay men represent themselves in public discourse: what gets said, how it gets stated, and what gets silenced. I search in this literature for moments of transgression, when gay men perform identities and practices that are counter to hegemonic heteronormative constructs. Ultimately, I search in the literature for answers to a series of questions that I carry with me on a daily basis:

- What can gay male identities and cultures offer the field of education?
- How can my performativity as a gay male college teacher rupture traditional forces that keep in place an oppressive status quo?
- What is my responsibility to my liberationist politics in my work as an educator and what kind of risk am I willing to take?

I visit my classroom where a number of incidents have left me pondering, reflective, but with little clarity or resolution. I use this series of events to illustrate dilemmas I have faced and the imperfect ways I have responded. These examples appear not because I seek to expose my own circumstance or to boldly bare my soul but because I believe other educators of varying identities face similar challenges. Through recounting these incidents, I aim to raise critical questions about the intersection of politics and teaching, identities and careers, self-care and courage.

Finally, drawing on the work of scholars of masculinities, I suggest places within discourses on gender, the body, and sexuality that offer opportunities for gay male teachers to fully recognize their potential contributions to the field of education and to the lives of children. My intent here is neither to produce an idealized, utopian (and intimidating) vision of what is possible nor to suggest that a singular path must be taken to fully integrate gay male identities in ways that allow the lover and the teacher within to inform each other. Instead my aim is to offer one possibility among many for allowing gay male teacher identities to emerge free from a burden of stigma and shame and to be fully able to play a transformative role in the social change work of education.

THE DISCOURSE OF GAY MALE TEACHERS

First-person narratives by gay male teachers usually reveal the trade-offs that lesbian, gay, bisexual, and transgender (LGBT) people are forced to make as they gain entry into broader arenas within the public sphere. As the gay drive to assimilate accelerates, it may be useful to consider what aspects of queer lives and cultures are deemed acceptable in mainstream (read "nongay") circles and what are cast out as unacceptable. These questions might be pondered not only by gay teachers but also by all openly LGBT people working outside specifically queered spaces. Likewise, these questions may be appropriately considered by other marginalized groups seeking entry into the status quo, who are also expected to cut off parts of themselves before being embraced as part of the American family.

Fundamentally, this is a question about democratic participation in the public sphere. When we in the United States say that we "value diversity," do we mean that we seek to create sites where people of different genders, races, classes, and sexual identities can come together and bring with them the social and cultural attributes that mark them as different, unusual, transgressive. Or do we mean that we like the *concept* of diversity but in practice aim to whitewash, silence, desex, straighten out, or overlook cultural differences? When white organizations seek to diversify, they frequently seek people of color who share their class, cultural, and ideological values. They grab at the African American corporate attorney, the female CEO, the assimilated Cuban physician, subsequently feeling smug about their new, diverse organization. They like the concept of diversity but are circumspect about creating situations where people truly have to work across profound social and cultural differences.

Some of us believe that only by engaging in sustained work across authentic differences can social change occur (Pharr 1996; Reagon 1983). We believe that the historical struggles of distinct groups have produced unique social patterns and cultural responses that have much to offer the world. We seek a multiculturalism that goes beyond "heroes and holidays," stretches further than ethnic potluck suppers, and is rooted in an authentic confrontation with difference (Lee, Menkart, and Okazawa-Rey 1997). From this vantage point, some gay men might usefully serve to complicate hegemonic understandings of the ways in which kinship patterns are structured, sexuality is enacted, and gender is performed.

The narratives of gay male teachers reveal that such contributions are not easily made. An analysis of Kevin Jennings's *One Teacher in 10: Gay and Lesbian Educators Tell Their Stories* (1994b) illustrates precisely the powerful challenges faced by gay male teachers who seek simply to survive in primary and postsecondary education in the United States. With stories of verbal harassment, physical assault, and threats of punitive action and job termination threaded throughout the volume, it seems impossible to imagine gay men having any breathing room in which they can assert transgressive aspects of gay male cultures. Not only are teachers—including queer teachers—a notoriously cautious and traditional lot (Lortie 1975), but the field of education is so intensely focused on social reproduction that pockets of resistance are few and far between (McLaren 1995). Add to these factors the very real threats that confront openly gay educators, and a risk-averse population is likely to be created. An English and Latin teacher in Saint Paul, Minnesota, John Pikala writes in Jennings's volume,

> My theme has been of a person, wounded by abandonment, who is a reluctant risk taker. I guess it is no surprise that some of us gay people, since we often face threatening situations, are hesitant about taking the risk of coming out. Gay teachers in particular feel that they are vulnerable; teachers as a group are probably the most deeply closeted segment of the gay community. We fear that, should we come out, we will lose, if not our jobs, at least the support and respect of our colleagues, superiors, students, and community. (93)

This explains, in part, the failure of gay male teachers to position themselves in relation to sex in anything other than heteronormative ways. With so much at stake simply by coming out, they imagine (perhaps appropriately) the earth cracking open and swallowing them up if they talk about sexual or romantic lives outside of a traditional committed dyad. Eleven of the twenty-three gay male contributors to this book reference their "partner" or "lover" or "life partner," whereas the others, for the most part, are silent about their sex and relational lives.

As historians and social critics have documented (D'Emilio and Freedman 1988; Rubin 1993; Seidman 1992), monogamy has been naturalized for heterosexuals in the United States. Yet the impeachment hearings surrounding President Clinton's extramarital sex exposed a gap between rhetoric and reality, even among Republican legislators backed by the Christian Right. With detailing Clinton's and Lewinsky's sexual tastes, newspapers "outed adultery," reporting the extramarital affair of U.S. Republican representative Henry Hyde, who chaired the House of Representatives impeachment hearings and for decades has been the champion of antichoice legislation; the affair that archconservative representative Helen Chenoweth had with a married man; and the extramarital affair of Speaker of the House–designate Robert Livingston (Keen and Chibbaro 1998). Although many heterosexuals apparently interpret the faithfulness clause in their marital vows as a commitment to avoiding sex with other partners, studies indicate that many violate these vows (Blumstein and Schwartz 1983), and the high rate of marital dissatisfaction and divorce suggests that organizing relationships around sexual monogamy might be unwise for some heterosexuals ("Marriage rate in U.S." 1999; "U.S. marriage" 1999).

In and of themselves, nonmonogamous relationships are not inherently emancipatory and may be as likely to reproduce unequal power relations between partners as monogamy does. Nor is nonmonogamy inconsistent with dominant sexual values ascribed to heterosexual masculinities and the accumulation of sexual "conquests." Yet failing to recognize nonmonogamous relationships as acceptable ways in which to organize sex and kinship functions to privilege monogamy and is critical to naturalizing it for heterosexuals. Jeffrey Weeks (1991) has grappled with this in the context of critiquing discourses of the "family":

> The real challenge lies not in attempting to find alternatives to the family, nor in attempting to make the term family so elastic that it embraces everything, and comes to mean nothing. On the contrary, the more dangerous and difficult task lies in the attempt to forge a moral language which is able to come to terms in a reasoned way with the variety of social possibilities that exist in the modern world, to shape a pluralistic set of values which is able to respect difference. (155)

The determinants for whether a relationship is oppressive or liberatory (or neither) are distinct from a narrow focus on monogamy/nonmonogamy; instead, the focus is on issues of open communication, consent, equality, and mutuality. Where nonmonogamy is not negotiated clearly and fairly or when agreements are violated or abused, inequities in the relationship are likely to be exacerbated.

Notwithstanding these provisos, what is problematic in the extreme is the erasure of nonmonogamous relationships from discussion of the everyday lives of gay male teachers and the privileging of discussion that creates a gay male social life to match a romanticized view of heterosexuality. For the most part, only when a gay teacher maintains a relationship that functions as a conceptual equivalent of the heterosexualized construct of a couple or a nuclear family does the relationship gain entry into Jennings's text. The gay male teacher narratives in this book lack references to any other form of sexualized male exchanges and authentic gay male community-based patterns of flirtations, casual sex, open relationships, or multipartnerism. On the page, at least, gay male teachers are not part of the leather scene, do not engage in sex in parks or highway rest areas, and do not trick out at their local bar on a Saturday night.

I say Pikala's quote explains in part this tendency to silence transgressive acts because sexual shame may be another force that delimits and restricts discussions of sex. One is tempted to probe behind some of the statements by the gay male teachers in this book. A San Francisco high school teacher captures a common response of many queer educators when faced with discussions about gayness:

> I don't think any teacher wants to initiate a conversation that leads to his or her students picturing them having sex, especially a type of sex which many still find revolting. (97)

A biology teacher in Cincinnati recounts his students' questions in response to his impromptu coming out:

> For the next thirty minutes I related my story and answered questions from my students, so many questions. "When did you know you were gay?" . . . "Does the principal know . . . ?" "How do you and your partner 'do it'?" . . . For the most part, the questions were an honest attempt to get some real answers. I was candid with them, but drew a line at privacy, my own and that of others. To questions of a sexual nature, I told them that those were personal, but that what goes on between two people of the same sex is not unlike a heterosexual couple. The important thing, I explained to them, is the love and caring that exists between the two individuals. (229–230)

Certainly many heterosexual students and faculty members continue to find gay male sex disgusting, but gay male teachers ourselves may also harbor powerful feelings of revulsion toward our sexual practices. The French sociologist Pierre Bourdieu has suggested that disgust should be "unpacked." What many naturalize as "good taste" emerges out of powerful social, economic, and cultural processes:

> Tastes (i.e., manifested preferences) are the practical affirmation of an inevitable difference. It is no accident that, when they have to be justified, they are asserted purely negatively, by the refusal of other tastes. In matters of taste, more than anywhere else, all determination is negation, and tastes are perhaps first and foremost distastes, disgust provoked by horror or visceral intolerance ("sick-making") of the tastes of others. . . . Aesthetic intolerance can be terribly violent. (Bourdieu 1984, 56)

When we insist that questions about sex acts remain privatized and when we support relegating them away from sites of public discourse, we may be buttressing an entire apparatus of social control that keeps in place patriarchy and heterosexism and makes common disgust for male-to-male sex. Some have argued that the relegating of sex to the private sphere is associated with many risks and that public sex functions in radical and liberating ways (Califia 1994; Dangerous Bedfellows 1996). Writing about gay men in particular, Michael Bronski (1996) has argued,

> We are obsessed with sex. And it's a good thing. Sexuality and eroticism are extraordinarily powerful forces in all our lives and gay culture acknowledges and supports that. . . . Mainstream culture is predicated upon repressing or denying sexuality. . . . Gay culture, by its insistence on the importance of sexuality, challenges this. (11–12)

The drive by gay male teachers to privatize our community's social and sexual practices raises a number of critical questions about how gay men consider and understand their social formations and sexual practices. Are kinships patterns that feature friendship networks or a sequence of three- to five-year-long primary relationships, ones in which we give ourselves permission to have outside sex, booby prizes foisted on us against our will by a homophobic culture? Or do we find meaning and pleasure in these arrangements? Do they work for us? Are promiscuity and casual sex a pathetic but understandable gay male cultural response to widespread societal persecution and the failure to have access to the institution of marriage, or can they be seen as life-affirming practices of bonding and exchanges of pleasure, intimacy, and affection? Our voices and gestures, our movements and inflections, the ones that violate gender norms and expose us as queer—are these the things we feel embarrassed about, even as we insist they have a right to exist without harassment or persecution? Or do we understand them as critically important forms of resistance to gender structures that otherwise produce male supremacy and reinforce patriarchal power?

I implicate myself in these same silences and denials. My own writings about my work as a gay male sixth-grade teacher reflect the same tendency toward silencing heretical sex, gender, and kinship constructs as *One Teacher in 10* does (Jennings 1994b). In 1985, I published a book about my first teaching job, the job that I lost after two years, when I came out of the closet. Reading my book *Socrates, Plato, and Guys like Me: Confessions of a Gay Schoolteacher* (1985) fifteen years later, I am struck by my reluctance to bring key aspects of gay culture and my emerging gay identity into the text. There are multiple allusions to visiting gay bars but always for seemingly chaste purposes. I visit Provincetown for a weekend, but there is no indication of my late-night visits to discos and leather bars. The only relationship that I acknowledge in the book is with a Catholic priest. In real life, this relationship was quite sexual and experimented with practices that were new to me, but the transformative nature of my relationship with "Tony Mosca" does not appear anywhere in the book. Instead I romanticize the relationship while I desex it:

> Loving a priest is not a picnic, but throughout the waning months of the year, I easily overlooked the problems. Sharing the Christmas holidays with Tony's clan was a special treat for me as I was learning to eat spicy Italian cooking and observe new ethnic customs. I envied the tacit acceptance of Tony's homosexuality by his family who—while never defining or categorizing or stating in words what was obvious—welcomed me as a son. And I was struck by the exhilaration of pulling blankets up over two big men on a cold winter evening and snuggling all night long. When Tony would tiptoe out at dawn to hurry to the seven o'clock mass, he'd kiss me on the forehead and set the alarm. I felt loved and cared for by another man—for the first time. (109)

The intense erotic connection I had with Tony is absent from the book, as are all the lessons he taught me about my body, desires, and spirituality (including bondage and discipline). Likewise, throughout the book, I perform traditional masculinity as a teacher and, while this was usually the way I appeared in the classroom at this time, I certainly had moments where I was caught gesturing or inflecting in effeminate and queeny ways.

These silences about gender and sex appear in other valuable books about lesbian and gay male teachers (Khayatt 1984; Kissen 1996). Why do we censor ourselves, and who benefits from the silences we create? When I reflect on the twenty-eight-year-old I was when I wrote *Socrates*, I cannot deny that my work in gay liberation at this time was powerfully transforming my understandings and relationships to sex and gender. Yet it seemed radical enough to be writing a book about being a homosexual teacher—including gender nonconformity or sexual liberation may have undermined my intended project. In my quest to show that I should be allowed to remain in the classroom as an openly gay teacher, I sacrificed parts of my identity that did not comfortably fit into the world's sense of what is appropriate conduct for a teacher.

I am struck these days by the continuing silences about sex and gender that continue to dominate discourses on gay male teachers. As a member of the Gay, Lesbian, and Straight Educators Network, I read monthly newsletters and see the programming at countless conferences for gay teachers. Yet I never see workshops for gay men who struggle to maintain integrity about the way we perform gender in the classroom (as we dodge spitballs) or read about resources for gay male teachers arrested during police raids on public sex areas. I subscribe to two computer listservs that frequently present interesting juxtapositions: one is a list that provides daily articles about gay issues in K–12 schools, and the other focuses on police crackdowns on public sex spaces throughout the nation. In stories published about the entrapment of men in park lavatories or highway rest areas, when the men's names and occupations are listed—a continuing problematic policy of many newspapers— there is almost always a schoolteacher or two in the mix. Do our gay teacher groups feel a responsibility to assist these teachers exposed to public scandal and potential job loss? Or is this aspect of these men's lives considered "conduct unbecoming" and relegated elsewhere?

CLASSROOM PREDICAMENTS NO. 1: ENACTING MASCULINITY

At various times in my college teaching career, I have become almost paralyzed with uncertainty about what to wear, how to speak, how to walk, how to sit, how to move. I neurotically obsess on these questions or repress them fully. I sometimes find myself spending as much time struggling over questions of appearance, voice, and movement as I do over the content of a day's lesson. Occasionally, on mornings when I teach, I open my closet and find not my clothes for the day but issues of whiteness, class status, gender performance, and sexual-identity enactment unleashed in a manner that threatens to overwhelm me and make me late for work.

When I am teaching my class Gay and Lesbian Issues in Schools, I am hyperaware of how I represent myself as a gay man to my students. I wonder how my queer students would like to see me perform gender and what my heterosexually identified students take away from their time with me. Should I look and act like a stereotypical fag, or should I provide an alternative vision of gay manhood? Is it okay to use camp, wit, and biting irony, or should I eschew the affectations of fagdom and provide an alternate vision? Is it okay to cross my legs, move my hands, raise my eyebrows? Can I call my gay students "honey"? Is it okay for me to refer to male colleagues as "girlfriends"? What image should I project when I walk across the room?

I feel as if biology has situated me in a somewhat privileged position to grapple with these questions. I possess key attributes that resonate with traditional masculinity in American culture: I am six feet four; I have thick facial and body hair; and I am built like a linebacker. I have taken what genetics has offered and made decisions that affix my position within masculine norms: I wear a beard, speak in a deep voice, keep my hair in a crew cut, and work out at a gym. I can easily perform a white ethnic masculinity common among working-class and lower-middle-class men. At times I look more like a stevedore than a schoolteacher.

Yet I am acutely aware that the masculinities I perform are cut through with political issues that can trigger a range of problematic responses. I may put on a performance of machismo at a local leather bar on a Saturday night, playing the big, tough butch man as a sexual strategy to signal a range of erotic activities and roles to the men I desire. Yet that same Village People macho man might make me seem intimidating and unapproachable to my undergraduate students and might suggest the affirmation of patriarchal norms that I actually aim to undermine. In one-on-one counseling situations with gay male students, I may cross my legs, affect a gentle voice, and make expressive hand gestures in an attempt to dissipate any sense of threats the students may feel from me. Yet the same display of "femme" energy might alienate many of my heterosexual students or confirm stereotypes. It also might undercut my ability as a teacher to structure the classroom, present expectations, and enforce standards for classroom discourse and student work. Should I resist affirming to students the typical stereotypes that say some gay men are effeminate?

When I first began to teach college, I found that the energy I project has a powerful influence on the response of students. I attempted to initiate empowering student-focused conversations utilizing my best critical pedagogy skills. Students worked with me to frame questions and organize classroom time. We planned format and process to maximize participation. Yet when time for discussion came, few students would participate. It sometimes felt as if I were pulling nails out of walls to get the majority of students to check in as part of the conversation.

One of the students—a women's studies major—was kind enough to approach me after one of my early failures at facilitating and encouraging a lively, engaged conversation. "The class is intimidated by you," she said matter-of-factly, shaking her head. "You say all the right things and clearly understand how these discussions are supposed to happen. Yet your energy—it's all wrong. It sends a very different message than the words you actually speak. You give off profoundly mixed signals."

I turned to colleagues for advice—lesbian colleagues, actually—who talked to me about gender performance in the classroom. They enlightened me about putting to work in my pedagogy my "butch" energies and my "femme" energies. At first I did not know what they meant, but I listened intently, took a lot of notes, and mulled their comments for quite a while. I realized that they were asking me to apply a valuable lesson to my undergraduate teaching, a lesson I had learned early in my career as a gay activist.

I have chaired many public forums, tense community meetings, and crisis-sparked town hall discussions where people of divergent views come together for debate, conflict, and resolution. When facilitating these events, I have learned to draw on different energies at different times. My butch energy, when channeled appropriately and nonabusively, is useful in setting limits, confronting participants who violate collectively made discussion rules, and keeping the group on task. I draw it from a place within me seeking to control, direct, and order. Although the gestures, inflections, and movements that accompany it may or may not look traditionally masculine, the energy definitely taps into that particular source within me.

My femme energy is employed to open up access, invite participation, and cut through and deflate tension. It employs humor, self-deprecation, campiness, and gentler qualities. I have become adept at recognizing when my femme energy will bring me things that my butch energy will not; I have some ability to dance between the two in a subtle but intricate performance of diversely gendered energies. I am also aware that my femme energy, when released properly, can be used effectively to set limits and keep an agenda on task.

I recognize that the use of constructs such as "butch" and "femme" can reinscribe essentialist views of gender. This is not my intent. I see neither term as natural or genetic, nor assigned by biology to one sex or the other. I share in Joan Nestle's understanding of the distinction between these terms and naturalized gender constructs:

> For me, "fem" has a very problematic relationship to "femininity"; perhaps because I spent my early lesbian years as a butchy-looking fem, perhaps because I have lived my whole adult life within lesbian communities, or perhaps because my mother wanted me to be more her missing husband than her sexually competitive daughter and thus gave me only rudimentary instruction in how to be a girl—wear a girdle or your ass will look like the side of a barn, wear lipstick so you don't look like death, always be a good fuck. (Nestle 1998, 129)

Hence while aware that such performances do not spring naturally from my maleness (Butler 1993), I deliberately and self-consciously have carried butch/femme energies into my classroom pedagogy. My women's studies student proved to be correct: When I introduce a class discussion gently, with openness and playfulness, and leave space for silences, humor, and the flexibility needed to accommodate last-minute student-initiated changes, my students respond enthusiastically. When I default to butch energies due to fear, disorganization, or mindlessness, the students usually are silent, frozen, sometimes even withholding.

I began to consider anew the male teachers I had known who had been explicitly effeminate, including music and drama teachers I had had during my high school years and one social studies teacher whose hands danced before him uncontrollably whenever something truly excited him. His enthusiasm proved infectious, and we students would become caught up in whatever passion he was creating in the classroom at that moment. Only after class, behind his back, would we mock him, call him names, and ridicule his style of teaching. Was this simply a case of his teaching methods' successfully capturing his students' interest, or was there something we truly loved about his campy gestures and queeny voice? Did these instances—moments of authentic pedagogical magic—allow teacher and students to collectively break out of constricted gender roles and, for at least a few minutes, violate patriarchal dicta?

Educators have started to write about how sexist and heterosexist practices in classrooms harm gender-nonconforming children, including boys and young men (Boldt 1997; Sedgwick 1993; Thorne 1993). Mairtin Mac an Ghaill (1994) has described schooling as a "masculinizing agency" and the "way in which dominant definitions of masculinity are affirmed within schools, where ideologies, discourses, representations and material practices systematically privilege boys and men" (4). R. W. Connell (1995) has argued that "a degendering strategy, an attempt to dismantle hegemonic masculinity, is unavoidable; a degendered rights-based politics of social justice cannot proceed without it" (232). He argues that schools must play a critical role in a move toward these politics:

> The importance of education of masculinity politics follows from the onto-formativity of gender practices, the fact that our enactments of masculinity and femininity bring a social reality into being. Education is often discussed as if it involved only information, teachers tipping measured doses of facts into the pupils' heads; but that is just part of the process. At a deeper level, education is the formation of capacities for practice. (239)

Clearly, gay male teachers have a great deal at stake in developing a "de-gendering strategy." Yet we are wrong if we pretend that our mere presence in the classroom, is counterhegemonic. Being transgressive because we are openly gay while being compliant because we affirm traditional masculinities may do little to alter the sex–gender system that wreaks havoc in our every-day lives.

CLASSROOM PREDICAMENTS NO. 2:
SEX, THE BODY, AND THE CLASSROOM

It is frightening to think about the relationship between one's sex life and one's classroom, between one's embodied identities as a teacher and a lover. Many gay men maintain sharp divides between the two, insisting one's sex life is personal and private and that it has no bearing on one's students. Yet the erotic circulates in any classroom and is often harnessed as a source of power that drives teaching pedagogies.

Like gay-identified men working in other mainstream cultural institutions—such as religious organizations, the health care industry, and the political arena—we as gay male teachers are offered two options: take a lover and perform with him a type of relationship that approximates hetero-coupledom; or desexualize ourselves, stifle our erotic energies, and disprove the stereotypes of the sex-obsessed homosexual. Gay male teacher identities rarely allow men room to construct personas that do not suppress the erotic and that allow them to avoid becoming leering, harassing letches who are inappropriate in a workplace. I worry that our performances within these narrow options present our gay male students—and others—with examples of gay identities that are neither helpful nor relevant to their lives and to the difficult choices they must face in integrating sexual identity, sexual orientation, and sexual energies into their personhood. Yet I take seriously concerns about power and consent that inform certain feminist thinking on sexual harassment (Dines, Jensen, and Russo 1998; Dworkin 1988; Frye 1983), and I believe that professors who address sex overtly in a classroom setting must be mindful of abuses and must be committed to self-scrutiny.

What possibilities exist for the creation of new kinds of gay male identity that acknowledge the value some of us place on the erotic and the ways in which it enters not only our classrooms and teaching practices but the classrooms and practices of all effective educators? If I take seriously many students' experiences of sexual harassment or abuse, it seems critical to examine my own sexualized persona rigorously and with tremendous sensitivity. Do we want to present ourselves to students as whole human beings—not simply as a mind but as a body, a spirit, and a sexuality? Is it possible to be seen by students as a sexual being without pandering to stereotypes or imposing one's comfort with sex onto students who maintain different values or who may have experienced harassment from teachers? As students struggle with their own sexual concerns, will I ever be able to find a way to support them without stifling my own struggles and silencing my own stories? How can a teacher from any vulnerable marginalized population even consider such questions without undermining her or his job and putting a career at risk?

I have faced a range of issues about sex, the body, and erotic desires during the three spring semesters in which I have taught my gay studies class:

- What do I do when I find in my mailbox on Valentine's Day a single long-stemmed rose that a staff member insists was placed there by "an unknown male undergraduate" who tried to deliver it surreptitiously?
- How do I respond when a student asks me if I will be dropping by the Bondage a Go-Go sex club on Wednesday night?
- When the weather gets warm and I am feeling good about my body, is it ever okay to wear a Lacoste shirt to class that shows my big arms? What about a tank top or simply a sleeveless vest?
- What should I do when I am cleaning up after a workout in the university recreation center's showers, and two of my undergraduate gay male students walk in and proceed to shoot quick glances in my direction as I quickly finish showering and toweling off?
- How do I react when I recognize a former or current student at a bathhouse, sex club, or while I am in a chat room on America Online?

The only conversations in this arena of which I have been a part have focused on the ethics of college teacher–student liaisons. I answered that question years ago for myself—deciding I did not need the risk and the headaches such interactions could bring—so perhaps this has allowed another series of questions to emerge for me. If I believe that there are many diverse and ethical ways for people to structure their social and sexual practices, is it important or educative to affirm various options within the classroom? Is it possible to affirm one pattern of sexual organization without undercutting others or violating critical boundaries that are intended to shield students from sexual harassment? What responsibility do gay male teachers who enjoy and intellectually support casual, nonmonogamous sexual relations have to our gay male students?

My students know that I have a lover and that I live with him in San Francisco. I introduce this tidbit—appropriately, I believe—during the first class, when I ask them not to call me at home after 9 PM. Several have met Crispin, either when we have run into students on the street or at gay community festivals and street fairs or when he has dropped in at our class potluck suppers. I am always acutely self-conscious of how I interact with my lover when students are around: I want to be "appropriate," but I do not want to fully stifle the attraction and physicality between us, nor do I want to elevate the erotic element of the relationship over others. When he visits me in class, I give him a peck of a kiss when I first see him, and I am conscious not to stifle touching his arm or holding his hand. If I run into students on the street when we are wearing tank tops or leather armbands, I become quite self-conscious, but I do not avoid greeting them nor do I feel ashamed to be seen or known to participate in gay male sexual cultures.

A few years back, a student drew an analogy in class that used my relationship with Crispin in a way that revealed how the student believed we were in a monogamous relationship. I cannot recollect the precise context for this incident, but it was something similar to a discussion I had recently had with students about the president's affair with Monica Lewinsky. During a heated discussion on this topic, one focusing on the role of Hilary Clinton, a student asked me, "How would you feel if Crispin were to have an affair with some other guy?"

In fact, I know how I would feel because our relationship is not sexually exclusive, and we regularly discuss our feelings about each other's "extramarital" liaisons. But how do I answer this question when it comes from undergraduate students who assume that being in a couple is automatically equated with monogamy?

When a student, Brenda, first raised a similar question in class and displayed her assumptions about the nature of our relationship and the boundaries about sex we had constructed, I paused for a moment and considered my response. It seemed as though an important, teachable moment had arrived but one fraught with all kinds of risks. Through my mind raced a number of scenarios: the dean confronting me with evidence that I had flaunted my sexual promiscuity to my students; a lawsuit where a group of students sue me for sexually harassing them by responding to Brenda's statement with anything other than "my sex live is my personal private business"; the newspaper headlines declaring, "He teaches at the university, but at night, he wallows in the sexual gutters of the naked city."

I paused before responding, then I downshifted energy and spoke directly to Brenda. "This might sounds strange for you to hear, but I feel as if I should correct an assumption that seems to lie behind your statement," I said calmly. "You seem to believe Crispin and I have structured our relationship in a manner that parallels traditional monogamous heterosexual relationships. Many couples—of all sexual orientations—choose other ways of organizing their relationship. It has been documented that gay men in particular often maintain what are known as open relationships. I just wanted you to know that your assumption doesn't fit our relationship design because we do not maintain monogamy in our relationship or believe we should control what our partner does with his body and his time. Open relationships surely have their challenges, but we've found it works best for us."

When I finished, there was total silence in the room. A few hands slowly were raised; additional students put forward some questions; I offered responses; then we returned to the lesson at hand. I felt conflicted between wanting to fully exploit a teachable moment and wanting to place what I believed were necessary boundaries on the discussion. Over the next few weeks, I heard from several students that they had appreciated my candor and the respect with which I held them, indicated by my disclosure. From that point forward, I believed that the class had become an intimate site for teaching and learning and that the rigid role of teacher had flexed in a way that promoted the critical pedagogy of the class.

I have had other encounters with my undergraduates that have challenged my commitment to including sex and the body in my teaching as something more than a distanced, depersonalized intellectual exercise. I have run into students at San Francisco's Folsom Street Fair, an annual event celebrating the leather and fetish communities, when we have all been dressed in sexualized clothing. Afterward, I have always believed it to be important to acknowledge the encounter before class in a casual, informal manner. Here I aim to show that participation in such activities is neither embarrassing nor a "big deal." One lesbian graduate student once referenced her interest in sadomasochism in a personal reflective paper, indicating that her own middle school students could deal with her lesbian identity but not her sexual interests. I thought it was appropriate and valuable to affirm her situation by sharing an incident from my own years as a middle school teacher, when students on the playground who were playing with handcuffs jokingly asked me if I had ever seen a pair. I indicated that I, too, owned a set of handcuffs and left it at that.

These teacher–student predicaments present distinct challenges related to whether one is teaching children or college students. Some insightful post-secondary educators have begun to examine the relationship between desire, love, and pedagogy (Barale 1994; Chapkis 1994; McWilliam and Jones 1996; Palmer 1996), but feminist scholar Jane Gallop has grappled most daringly with the relationship between desire, sexuality, and pedagogy—first in *Thinking through the Body* (1988), where, drawing on Sade, she makes connections between pederasty and pedagogy, particularly at the college level:

> Pederasty is undoubtedly a useful paradigm for classic European pedagogy. A greater man penetrates a lesser man with his knowledge. The student is empty, a receptacle for the phallus; the teacher is the phallic fullness of knowledge. The fact that teacher and student are traditionally of the same sex but of different ages contributes to the interpretation that the student has no otherness, nothing different from the teacher, simply less. (43)

More recently, in her *Feminist Accused of Sexual Harassment* (1997), Gallop explores her experience as "a feminist professor who was accused by two students of sexual harassment" (1). Insisting that her coming of age in the feminist movement of the 1970s has led her to "not respect the line between the intellectual and the sexual" (12), Gallop discusses the excitement she hopes to create in her classroom:

> Sometimes a class or some more informal gathering suddenly comes together, and I feel the electricity, the buzz of live knowledge, the excitement of women thinking freely together. I always try to get us to that place where learning begins to dance. When we get there, my students love me and I'm crazy for them. (20)

Gallop argues that expunging sex and desire from classroom teaching and from consensual teacher–student relations dehumanizes pedagogy:

> Telling teachers and students that we must not engage each other sexually ultimately tells us that we must limit ourselves to the confines of some restricted professional transaction, that we *should not treat each other as human beings*. (51)

For Gallop, excellent teaching is about love and desire, and she argues that current regulations diminish not only the humanity of teachers and students but also the quality of education:

> At its most intense—and, I would argue, its most productive—the pedagogical relation between teacher and student is, in fact, a "consensual amorous relation."

And if schools decide to prohibit not only sex but "amorous relations" between teacher and student, the "consensual amorous relation" that will be banned from our campuses might just be teaching itself. (57)

Gallop raises a host of valuable issues; however, after a thorough reading of her work I am unclear about how to "operationalize" her thinking. I neither wish to overstate or be paralyzed by the realities of sexual power inequalities between students and teachers, nor do I wish to trivialize or ignore them. Likewise, I become confused about what exactly might be an "appropriate" response to the reality of emotional intimacy and sexuality in the teacher–student relationship. Setting my own boundaries here has relieved me greatly, yet the larger intellectual and ethical questions remain unanswered.

Parallel issues emerge when examining desire and sex in early childhood, primary, and secondary education, but the tensions are different and the taboo is even greater. In a powerful essay titled "Classroom Management and the Erasure of Teacher Desire," Anne Phelan (1997) examines ways in which the "preoccupation with orderly conduct in schools" masks "a disciplining of student and teacher desires, bodies and pleasures." Phelan attributes the obsessive preoccupation with order to "a fear of the erotic" and shows how teachers and children pay a price for our cultural erotophobia:

> Teachers are in fear that their touch may be framed as molestation, their emotional expression as professionally inappropriate. The downside is that teachers are in danger of forgetting their capacity for feeling. (89)

Jonathan Silin, writing in *Sex, Death, and the Education of Children: Our Passion for Ignorance in the Age of AIDS* (1995), tackles the issue of "educational pederasty" in a manner similar to Gallop's. Yet, because Silin's site of inquiry is the early childhood classroom, he confronts "assumptions of innocence" and "issues of protection and control that form the boundaries of the childhood closet" (202). Arguing that current organization of early childhood programs "deny the sexuality of both adults and children" (203), Silin makes explicit that the child as innocent and the homosexual as pervert are conjoined constructs keeping in place a range of social norms, policing tactics, and destructive power relations. James King's work (1998) on male early childhood teachers shows how these power relations manifest themselves most powerfully through gender and sexual orientation and serve as barriers to men's participation in teaching and the enactment of particular forms of caring. In *Schooling Sexualities* (1998), Debbie Epstein and Richard Johnson provide rich data from teenage students in British schools that illustrate the ways in which schools shape sexualities and structure sexual hierarchies.

Their book reveals the profound sexual cultures of schools, even during a period in British educational policy that has attempted to increasingly regulate and repress sex education, sexual diversity, and sexual freedom.

As I consider my own classroom predicaments, I realize that my aim in confronting issues of desire, sex, and love in my pedagogy and relations with students is not to get into trouble, violate valuable boundaries protecting students from harassment, or earn a reputation as a particularly transgressive or radical educator. Instead I believe that the stigmatizing, silencing, scapegoating, and attacks that commonly surround the appearance of sex in the classroom are social practices that contribute to producing a populace that experiences sex and desire in a manner best characterized by confusion, frustration, pain, and abuse. If critical pedagogy is about collectively gaining a deep understanding of how social and political forces interact with all of our everyday lives and help to produce our identities, social practices, and communities, then silencing, avoiding, or depersonalizing/disembodying sex may function powerfully to affirm and reify a dangerous and oppressive status quo.

REPRODUCING OR RE-CREATING THE BODY POLITIC?

Silin (1997) argues that "Americans are alternately expansive and silent about the place of sexuality in the early childhood classroom" (214). The intense obsession with sex and schooling and the profound silences associated with it are part of an ideology that is effective at, as James Sears (1992) has aptly stated, "reproducing the body politic" (15). Keeping sex private and silencing discussion of desire, bodies, and erotic practices in classroom discourse effectively ensures the continued marshaling of sex as an effective form of social control. As Sears states,

> Sexuality, then, is more a construct of ideology and culture than it is a collection of information about biology and the body; power and control are central to our modern understanding of sexuality and ourselves as sexual beings. . . . How we define and express our sexuality has significant political implications. . . . There is, then, an integral relationship between the learning of human reproduction and reproduction of social relations. Understandings of gendered and sexual arrangements, teenage pregnancy, and child sexual abuse further illustrate this relationship. (18–19)

As teachers, we all teach a great deal about sex, whether we acknowledge it or not. What we say and what we do not say, what is voiced and what is silenced create knowledges for our students with tremendous ramifiications. Gay male teachers—whose bodies, desires, and practices may transgress heteronormative constructs and patriarchal paradigms—could be a source of startling new learnings. This chapter represents an initial attempt to trouble the comfortable notions of gay male teachers that circulate within liberal educational discourse. I have attempted to examine ways in which gay male identities and cultures might be useful in our pedagogical practices.

For too long, gay men have understandably fought a narrow battle, seeking admittance into the classroom as openly gay educators. Likewise, queer students of all genders and sexualities have worked to achieve a relative degree of safety in public schools throughout the United States. All too often, as we have made these efforts, we have made compromises and sacrifices that have gone unspoken and unacknowledged. We have gained limited entry into the classroom by denying authentic differences between many gay men's relationships to gender roles, sexual cultures, and kinship arrangements and those of the heteronormative hegemony.

This chapter is a call to dialogue about the sacrifices we have made and the implications they have for democratic education and social change.

7

Desires as Defiance: Transgression, Risk Taking, and Resistance to Safe-Sex Education

My sexual desires are usually linked to transgression. While some people organize their erotic impulses around a safe and cozy domesticity, I move toward what is forbidden and dangerous. I am drawn to not by what is clean and tidy but by what is dirty and messy. I am enticed by what is risky, vanished, or exiled, not by what's safe and socially celebrated. For me, sexual fantasy and activity are closely linked to the taboo, as if my carnal yearnings are linked to flouting conventions, challenging social expectations, and defying cultural norms.

I do not think that I am unusual. When I look at cultural products marketed to stimulate desire—items ranging from romance novels and daytime soap operas to magazines such as *Playboy* or *Hustler*—I notice the focus on transgressing boundaries and resisting social norms. Whether it is the soap operas featuring married men engaging in secret affairs with their secretaries or the pinup girl wearing spiked heels and holding a whip, these texts suggest that simple domesticity and narrow cultural conformity do not carry a huge erotic charge. What is sexy does not seem to be purity but the desecration of purity. Unless boundaries get violated—unless we move from the mainstream to the margin or over the edge—our culture cannot get off.

At the same time, I do not believe everyone organizes his or her sex in this way. While I might seek out partners from populations who violate the social expectations placed on people of my social location (I seek men rather than women; I seek working-class men rather than middle-class men) or engage in sexual activities considered taboo (promiscuity or sadomasochism, for example), many people clearly find pleasure and sexual fulfillment with partners and activities that do not transgress status quo social expectations. When I recently heard a colleague, one who shares this connection between desire and transgression, suggest that long-term married couples enjoy a lively sex life only by fantasizing about other partners or by bringing taboo into their erotic activities, I disagreed. Extrapolating our organization of desire to the entire population seems arrogant and without evidence.

SEXUAL SUBJECTIVITY AND RESISTANCE TO SOCIAL NORMS

Cultural messages and social institutions encouraged me from a young age to organize my sexual desires around "love," a vague and underexamined term that held out the promise of "one true love" in exchange for immersing myself in the culture of romance. I saw movies, read books, listened to rock music, and enjoyed television situation comedies that directed me into managing my emotions and desires narrowly: I was encouraged to "fall in love" with a woman of my same race and class, marry, and procreate. Feminist and cultural studies scholars have documented the powerful ways in which social and cultural forces have conspired to create a patriarchal culture of romance (Holland and Eisenhart 1990; Seidman 1991, 1992), enforce heterosexuality (Rich 1983), and regulate sexual desires and practices (Rubin 1984).

If one does not believe that the landscape of one's sexuality is genetically or biologically determined (including one's sexual orientation, partner choice, erotic preferences, and fetishes) or that sexuality narrowly emerges out of individualized psychological and familial dynamics (Archer 1999; Fausto-Sterling 2000; Scarce 1999a; Terry 1999; Whisman 1995), what alternative explanations are available? If one looks critically at naturalized understandings of sexuality, such as "I'm gay because I was born that way" or "Growing up with an absent father made me homosexual," is the only alternative to argue that social and cultural forces determined the directions of one's sexual interests? Can we carve out an understanding of the genesis of our desires, practices, and identities that involves an element of choice? Does sexual subjectivity allow for agency?

Despite this powerful drive to steer the masses as sheep being shepherded in specific directions, resistance emerges alongside compliance. When the engines of the culture universally aim to imprint bodies and desires with the mark of heterosexuality, some fraction of the population moves toward homosexuality; when the masses are powerfully encouraged to distinguish between the sexes and to organize desire in monosexual ways, some portion of the populace will resist and move toward bisexuality and defiance of rigid gender norms. If vaginal intercourse between a married, male–female couple in so-called missionary position is culturally privileged (Rubin 1984), is it any surprise that many—or most—people are instead powerfully drawn to oral sex, anal sex, and sex outside of matrimonial vows?

Hence, lesbians, gay men, bisexuals, and transgenders may be rebellious by-products of culture's drive toward sexual and gender conformity. Likewise, we find people whose extramarital affairs bring with them a special charge because they are culturally forbidden. We can identify middle-age men pursuing women half their age and people who fetishize race, ethnicity, or socioeconomic class. For many, the forbidden becomes desired; taboo produces cravings; the return of the repressed is made corporeal and is experienced as an enormous hunger.

Would the individuals within these specific populations—lesbians, married people engaged in extramarital affairs, people involved in intergenerational relationships—identify themselves as "cultural resisters" if asked? Would they claim identities as "sexual renegades"? Would they acknowledge ownership and pride in their outlaw desires?

Probably not, particularly during a cultural moment in which increasingly diverse practices and ways of being have been naturalized, biologized, or geneticized (Scarce 1999a). More likely they would default to a simple explanation: "I was born this way." Whether discussing sexual orientation, preferences for specific sex acts, powerful erotic fantasies, or the ways our sex is organized, we are encouraged to respond as if desires are hardwired into our bodies. As one man I met recently told me, "I'm into leather because I was born this way."

Hence individuals whose sexualities are organized around transgression face a stark explanatory choice: they can choose biology and maintain that they were genetically driven to be gay (or enjoy sex with multiple partners, or prefer kinky sex), or they can opt for a social and psychological explanation and insist that they were raised in a setting that produced them as gay.

Few seem willing to consider their own volition in the production of desires, fantasies, and practices. Does something or someone else organize my sexual subjectivity, or do I have a portion of agency that actively allows me to proceed in certain directions and not others? Does my "choice" to be a gay man fall along the same axis as my "choice" for kinky sex? Am I simply someone who opts for the outlaw category in all erotic areas? Or was I born defiant and can thus excuse my kinks and twists as "not my fault"? These questions, considered through the work of the late French sociologist Pierre Bourdieu (1982), might emerge as, Does my identity as a gay man emerge from a preexisting outlaw habitus? Or does my identity as a sexual outlaw emerge from a preexisting gay habitus?

EDUCATION, HEALTH PROMOTION,
AND CHILDHOOD DEFIANCE

How does a subculture's relationship to the taboo affect that group's relationship to education, health, and safety? What would it mean if some people came to define themselves as queers, lesbians, or gay men not because of a specific gene but because on some level—a level different from that of conscious and rational choice (Bourdieu 1984)—these people organized their gender and sexual identities as acts of resistance to the status quo? What would it mean for some young men to direct their desire toward other males as a strategy of circumventing the institutions of heterosexuality, patriarchal masculinities, or an antipleasure culture? How would our work with health promotion and HIV be transformed if many gay men—or many people of all genders and sexual identities—constituted their sexual subjectivities in part out of a deep-seated impulse of resistance?

My own coming-of-age odyssey in the 1960s and 1970s suggests that looking at sexual subjectivities through this lens may produce useful possibilities. For instance, from age five or six, I began to avoid the rough and tumble of sports and boy culture in favor of jumping rope and playing house with the girls; some might see this as evidence that I was homosexual or at least gender nonconforming from an early age. Despite my father's insistence that I play baseball and despite other adults' overt disapproval of my activities and girlish ways, I risked social approbation and parental punishment to sneak away and play hopscotch. When viewed through superficial contemporary explanations for the genesis of sexuality, this is evidence enough to prove that I was born homosexual.

Such activities, however, could just as easily be seen as indications of a strong-willed and strategic child who willfully violated social norms because of his assessment of the political underpinnings of boy culture. In my six-year-old fashion, I noted the power dynamics, read the cultural semiotics, and opted out.

Cultural messages exclaiming that *real* boys played sports, that gentle gender-nonconforming boys were sick or sinful, and that girl culture was unimportant and without social value could be considered a form of "health promotion" directed toward my boy self. My father's anguished talks attempting to persuade me to be a "real" boy and play basketball with him could be understood as a father–son health intervention. Health promotion was at the core of the second-grade teacher's phoning my mother because I was spending my free time baking pretend pies in our classroom's Easy-Bake oven. Most powerfully, health promotion may have been directed at me by the gangs of boys who would taunt and bully me, chiding me to walk, gesture, cross my legs, and inflect my words in gender-conforming ways.

Could these activities, messages, and rituals be understood as promoting my health and safety by coercing me into a traditional gender identity? If I would only accede to this particular health promotion campaign—rather than stubbornly resist—I would not have that bruise under my eye, the ever-present terror of the bully, and the extra twenty pounds around my waistline.

As I entered adolescence, becoming one within the age group commonly viewed as being particularly needy of safety education and health promotions, I was met with a series of new interventions. This pivotal and problematic life stage is seen as offering prime opportunities for health promotion activities related to diet, exercise, automobile safety, substance use, and sexual conduct. Thus, Boy Scout handbooks provided boys like me with basic first-aid technique but also warned us about playing with knives, experimenting with matches, or venturing alone into unknown wilderness areas. Health classes in junior high schools forced our eyes to view graphic films filled with the evidence of what happens to inebriated teenagers who get behind the wheel of a car, fall under the influence of the evil weed, or engage in the evils of masturbation.

We came to know precisely how we were expected to rhetorically respond when tested on our knowledge of these health risks or when questioned by our parents. Did these campaigns succeed at leading us to chasten our ways, or did something more complicated occur? Could these activities have served to introduce us to a range of previously underconsidered possibilities marked by risk and danger that our teenage subjectivities experienced in diverse and unpredictable ways? In what ways did adolescent health promotion—and the biases and power dynamics contained within these campaigns—serve merely to brand specific activities and social practices as "cool" and others as "nerdish"?

When teen health promotion intersects with teen subjectivities, does a simple, linear equation of HAZARD + WARNING = DETERRANT result? Or could some adolescents "choose" other options, such as HAZARD + WARNING = ATTRACTION or HAZARD + WARNING = HAZARD × HAZARD? In what ways did my already-perfected best-little-boy-in-the-world persona function simply to disguise my dawning move toward outlaw status? Did my values collude with a maturing sense of personal agency to create a decision-like strategic process resulting in my embracing precisely those activities from which health promotion was attempting to scare me away?

Could my incipient binge drinking in high school be understood not simply as a mindless, uncritical "adolescent rebellion" but as a choice to defy the infantilization of an age cohort of people who cross-culturally and transhistorically have been granted the privileges and status of adulthood? (Aries 1965). Was my eventual dabbling in drugs in college triggered by a kind of resistance to the class and age biases included in this health promotion? At precisely the moment I was instructing my body to transgress almost two decades of dictates and fully enact my rebellious sexual desires, was I also choosing to resist the dictates of other brands of health promotion?

With this narrative, I am asking the reader to consider that sexual desires, preferences, and practices may not be driven by forces traditionally called on to distribute responsibility for deviance—namely, inherent biology, narrow familial patterns (weak father / strong mother), and overwhelming social and cultural forces. Instead I am suggesting that a form of selection might take place outside the realm of rational choice that is best understood as rooted in alternative ideals and counterhegemonic ethics. Rather than see my gender-nonconforming self or my homosexuality as rooted in deficits (e.g., a lack of effective male role models), could they be understood as forms of resistance to the values incorporated in traditional masculinities or the heteronormative sex–gender system? (Connell 1995; Rubin 1984) Could I—could all queer youth—actually be active agents in moving into their queer identities and lives?

So often when queers are faced with the smug Christian who questions why they would "make the choice to be homosexual," we respond by saying, "Who would choose to be homosexual? With all the discrimination and violence directed at LGBT people, why would anyone in their right mind make a choice to be gay?" Two things have long interested me about this clichéd exchange: first, that the Christian has clearly experienced his or her sexual orientation as a matter of choice and on some level is acknowledging that he or she has experienced same-sex attractions; second, that the gay person, on summing up the pluses and minuses of his or her life experience as a queer, wishes to have turned out heterosexual. Yet isn't it possible that many of us moved toward the gay side of life because we sensed it offered us valuable experiences and meaningful opportunities?

On a cultural level, a vast amount of so-called health promotion takes place to produce a population that sees itself as monosexual, understands the sexes as "opposites," and directs erotic impulses to the other sex. This kind of health promotion is woven fully into the apparatus of the culture and finds its way into countless cultural products, social institutions, and everyday social practices. Throughout my childhood and adolescence, aspects of the cultural apparatus colluded in a powerful attempt to overdetermine me as masculine and heterosexual.

Constructed much like contemporary American antismoking campaigns were the illustrations of masculinity in *Sports Illustrated* or my Boy Scout manual, which powerfully functioned to send a clear signal of how to act and how not to act; warnings and threats by my parents served the same purpose as did the labeling on cigarette packaging (HAZARDOUS TO YOUR HEALTH); the absence of lesbians and gay men from the public sphere functioned as does today's ban on tobacco use in restaurants and bars. Powerful cultural efforts demand all of us to avoid tobacco use, yet still some young people "choose" to smoke. With all images of gender nonconformity and homosexuality mocked, derided, and exiled from the pubic sphere in the 1950s and 1960s, I still moved toward men. Evidence of no options (biology) or a powerfully resistant sense of entitlement and agency?

What I remember most are three things about the years before my consciousness evolved an adult intellect and an ability to rationally reflect: a disdain for a pecking-order social world of competition and power abuse; an appreciation for forms of social organization valuing nurturance and cooperation; and a keen, strategic ability to negotiate through the social worlds in which I was situated with subtle defiance and an entitlement to a concordance between my values and my emerging identities.

What would it mean for health promotion if who we regard today as "gay men" were actually a grown-up tribe of active resisters to heteronormative and patriarchal values? How might this possibility challenge the assumptions behind social-marketing campaigns and other forms of health promotion that disregard the concept of resistance? In what ways might a large strain of resistance within this particular population's constitution, social relations, and landscapes of desire function to undermine, complicate, or throw some surprising convolutions into these efforts?

IS HEALTH PROMOTION PLACING GAY MEN AT INCREASED RISK?

I have written extensively about ways in which health promotion focused on safe sex and HIV prevention for gay men may have resulted in the production of precisely the desires and activities that such efforts were intended to diminish (Rofes 1996, 1998a). I have wondered whether twenty years of "use a condom every time" messages did not serve to move sodomy from margin to center in the gay male sexual imaginary. With a barrage of health promotion messages repeatedly flashing before our eyes through magazine advertisements, billboards in gay enclaves, lapel buttons and T-shirts, banners in gay pride marches, posters at sex venues, and safe-sex packets distributed at health conferences, how did we respond? Did these activities truly fit the Geneva Convention's understanding of health promotion as "the process of enabling people to increase control over, and to improve, their health"? (World Health Organization 1996). As a gay man with little interest in anal intercourse before the epidemic and as one with a large interest after such prevention efforts, did health promotion elicit an unexpected response from my sexual subjectivity closely linked to transgression, defiance, and taboo?

When safe sex campaigns began in the United States and clarified that risk was most closely associated with anal sex, I felt fortunate: the danger was contained in an act that did not appear on my "top ten list" of sexual activity preferences and one in which I rarely participated as either a "top" or a "bottom." I recall questioning whether HIV prevention efforts should count me as among those they had "saved" from infection because the primary route of transmission was not within my sexual repertoire. I could easily wear a button back then claiming "Good Gay Men Practice Safe Sex 100%" because, to me, this took little effort and exacted no price.

By the late 1980s, American HIV prevention leaders insisted that the gay populace had been educated and had fully transformed its sexual practices. Some AIDS education programs actually shut their doors, considering their work complete. Personal advertisements in gay publications during these years contained no references to unprotected anal sex, and typical social banter among gay men included the assumption that everyone was practicing safe sex all the time. Anal sex absent a condom had become a forbidden act that gay men publicly renounced in exchange for an identity as a socially responsible gay man. As Peter Keogh has asserted, a previously despised population was extended citizenship in exchange for repudiating the forbidden act (Keogh 2001).

Not only did safe-sex campaigns function to create a hegemonic view of "acceptable" gay male sexual activity, but these health promotion campaigns may have also included elements that functioned as triggers for resistance. Does the inclusion of "safe" in the term "safe sex" make this seem like a hot and exciting activity to pursue, or does it simply serve to diminish the heat surrounding the suggested act? Does a population that has already opted for risk over safety (via gender and sexual identity) consider "safe" equivalent to "status quo," "heteronormative," or "boring" and hence move toward the unsafe? Does an appeal to safety and social responsibility as central to these campaigns actually spark a counterresponse from many gay men, especially those gay men who overtly adopt renegade identities and subcultural norms?

Some HIV prevention groups appear to regard barebacking, the eroticized practice of anal sex without condoms, as a militant resistance to the colonization of a community's sexuality:

> In the last few years gay men have gotten serious about the right to fuck without condoms. After all, practically every straight guy in the world gets to do it without being told they are irresponsible, foolish, suicidal, or homicidal. A lot of guys think we should have the same right. *Barebacking is a right. . . . Barebacking is liberation. . . . Barebacking is defiance.* (San Francisco AIDS Foundation 2000a)

As gay men, do we somehow intuit biases against our sexual values and sex cultures in health promotion that hearken back to the ways in which health promotion during our childhoods and teen years seemed determined to steer us into traditional heteronormative masculinities? Peter Keogh raises important questions about the politics of health promotion that powerfully confront what we may be facing:

> When health-seeking behaviors are to be encouraged, such as avoiding the transmission of HIV through sexual contact, the opposed notions of coercion versus voluntarism come into play. Questions emerge: should choice and individual self-determination be promoted at the expense of larger epidemiological imperatives? How is health and choice to be promoted? When these questions are asked about a group to whom choice and freedom have traditionally been denied and where the disease in question threatens to stigmatize those who contract it, these questions become particularly poignant. (Keogh 2001, 3)

When barebacking emerged on the American scene in the late 1990s, some argued that such a renegade movement should have been expected as a backlash against fifteen years of gay men's being dominated by a brand of health promotion that they characterized as simplistic, patronizing, disempowering, sexphobic, and homophobic (Elovich 1999; Scarce 1999b, 1999c). The silence surrounding unprotected anal sex was briefly replaced by a period of burgeoning discourse within the queer public sphere, focused on bareback sex parties (where condoms are not permitted), the risk of ever forgoing condom use, and the websites extolling the glories of exchanging semen. Did the emerging debates serve to resolve issues of risk and safety or simply affirm to the masses of gay men what they already knew: that anal sex and semen exchange are the "hot" act for today's sexual outlaw?

IS THERE MUCH NEW ABOUT THE NEW WAVE OF HIV EDUCATION?

During recent years a series of HIV prevention campaigns for gay men have appeared in the United States, Australia, and England in the pages of gay publications and in posters, brochures, and websites. Considered a "new stage" of HIV education, these campaigns created much public debate for stepping beyond the "use a condom every time" efforts of the 1980s and 1990s. These campaigns included Terrence Higgins Trust and Community HIV and AIDS Prevention Strategy's *Facts for Life* and *In Two Minds?* campaigns, in England (2001a, 2001b); Gay Men Fight AIDS's *Enjoy Fucking?* and *Bareback* campaigns, also in England (2001, 2002); the AIDS Council of New South

Wales's *Give a Fuck* campaign (2000); the San Francisco AIDS Foundation's *The New Epidemic* campaign, a four-part advertisement series; and San Francisco's Stop AIDS Project's *HIV Stops with Me* campaign.

All of these efforts are focused on high-quality visuals and powerfully explicit texts. Most feature graphics depicting gay men, including several campaigns that use photographs of a diverse collection of "regular" gay men. The campaigns seem to share a desire to avoid being explicitly prescriptive or directive and instead model what Peter Keogh (2001) has aptly cited as the "normative" (14):

> They illustrate healthy ways of being. The significance of this shift from prescription to normativity cannot be underestimated. Health promotion now constructs gay men as no longer intrinsically risky individuals, but rather sees them as having a capacity to manage risk. . .As health promotion seeks to regulate by means of incentive rather than censorship, it talks about more than behaviors, engaging instead in a socially constructed task that goes to the heart of the individual. This might be defined as promoting gay citizenship. (14–15)

A review of these efforts—intended in part to respond to barebacking and reports of upswings in sexually transmitted infections—suggests that HIV education efforts may continue to be operating out of the same problematic assumptions, manipulating gay men's desires and practices in uncertain ways, and producing the precise activities they were created to counter. The shift away from prescription, however welcome, may benefit no one if the privileged alternative is participation in a sanitized, wholesome gay citizenship. For gay men whose sexualities include an element of transgression, this might simply offer a different target against which to rebel.

I maintain three major concerns about these ambitious efforts. First, the HIV prevention campaigns continue health promotion's two-decade tradition of emphasizing anal sex, sending an implicit message that this is not only the primary sexual activity bearing risk for transmitting HIV for gay men but the preeminent and most desirable act within the sexual repertoire of the gay male populace. AIDS Council of New South Wales's *Give a Fuck* campaign attempts to play off the multiple meanings of the word "fuck" yet simultaneously hammers home through language and explicit graphics that fucking is the ultimate act of gay male sexuality. Likewise, Gay Men Fight AIDS's *Enjoy Fucking?* campaign includes three powerful visuals, all highly stylized images of two men fucking. The observer's eye is drawn to the words *Enjoy Fucking?* as the uppermost text with the largest typeface on the advertisement. Although the follow-up line—"You Can Reduce the Risk!"—is intended to direct the viewer to consider prophylactic measures, the emphasis on *Enjoy Fucking?* seems likely to buttress a cultural norm that one *should* enjoy this particular act and that one may be less of a man (or less of a gay man) if one does not share a significant interest in anal sex.

Second, all of these campaigns are focused on barebacking—anal sex without condoms—yet continue to be explicitly designed as condom campaigns. An activity occurring without a condom is intruded on repeatedly by condom discourse. All eight of Terrence Higgins Trust and Community HIV and AIDS Prevention Strategy's *Facts for Life* posters close with the line, "It's worth remembering that condoms, used properly, stop HIV." Likewise, AIDS Council of New South Wales's *Give a Fuck* campaign posters close with the line, "Using a condom and lube is the safest way to have casual anal sex." Gay Men Fight AIDS's *Enjoy Fucking?* campaign advertisements end with the line, "Condoms and plenty of water-based lube still provide the safest fuck." And every one of Terrence Higgins Trust and Community HIV and AIDS Prevention Strategy's *In Two Minds?* posters that include text repeatedly highlights condoms. Although the designers of these campaigns may have attempted to shift from the prescriptive, "Use a condom every time" message to the less explicit directive of "It's worth remembering that condoms, used properly, stop HIV," the intrusion of condoms into the text and the repeated use of a tag line that seems almost parental (even patronizing) make these efforts less of a departure than they perhaps appear.

Third, all of these campaigns attempt to offer individual gay men a nuanced trade-off that may be much more complicated than the campaigns' designers are willing to face. These campaigns reflect a shift in social norms away from earlier efforts that categorized all acts of anal sex without condoms as unacceptable toward efforts categorizing certain acts of anal sex without condoms as unacceptable, such as barebacking between two men of different antibody status (one is HIV positive and one is HIV negative) and barebacking between two lovers who are negative and not in a monogamous relationship. However, they continue to rely on categorization of sex acts and sexual actors as "good" and "bad." In Stop AIDS's *HIV Stops with Me* campaign, we are offered repeated images of the "good" HIV-positive person, which encourage viewers to imagine the counterpart—the "bad" HIV-positive person. Gay Men Fight AIDS's clever and graphically original *Bareback* campaign produces three advertisements focused on the gay man who is "negative and so is my boyfriend," the HIV-positive man who enjoys barebacking but "only with other positive men," and the HIV-positive man who does not ever bareback ("It's not worth the worry"). San Francisco AIDS Foundation's barebacking advertisement in their *New Epidemic* campaign asks, "If we're going to bareback, can we do it without fucking over everything else?" Again, the appeal is to barebackers to be "good gay citizens" and put social responsibility ahead of personal preferences, pleasure, or meaning.

Although the sentiment here is nice and I share in the desire for all people to embrace social responsibility, what I am questioning is whether such efforts actually lead to fewer acts of unprotected anal sex.

These seven campaigns are considered by many to be part of a daring and progressive new era of health promotion; but by failing to consider a resistant impulse within many gay men's sexual subjectivities, they may actually be implicated in perpetuating the very activities they aim to diminish. By continuing to single out anal sex and address it outside a context of other sexual activities, they may continue to be producing increased desire for this act. By making the slight shift from prescriptive directives about condom use to suggestive directives about condom use, they may generate a rebellious dislike or an overt hostility to the cumbersome nature of condoms and to the attempt to colonize gay men's most intimate sexual practices. By continuing to function as arbiters of the morality of specific sex acts and specific gay men and by refusing to move entirely beyond the paradigm of authority and judgment, these campaigns may continue to trigger reactions of resistance rather than compliance. Without questioning the ethics and politics of producing a "goodie" and "baddie" gay man, such campaigns may be experienced by many gay men as simply the latest installment in a lifetime of problematic relationships with health promotion.

VEXING QUESTIONS

In an article providing information about the *New Epidemic* campaign, the San Francisco AIDS Foundation newsletter explains, "The purpose of the ads is to capture the attention of our target population and stimulate some new thinking about complex issues." (San Francisco AIDS Foundation 2000b).

If "thinking" and rational choice decision making are the primary activities that determine the sexual activities of most gay men, then information-based interventions that offer new data, new perspectives, and new possibilities might be the best way to reduce unprotected anal sex. If most gay men do not share a significant element of resistance in their response to health promotion, then this new wave of prevention efforts might achieve great success. Yet if this resistant element is present in a large portion of the population targeted by these campaigns—or if most sex emerges in a manner separate from rational choice—the efforts might result in increasing the precise activities they are attempting to diminish.

Astute critics have raised questions about ways in which traditional health promotion might face special challenges with HIV prevention:

Sexual health promotion can be difficult in many settings in which other health promotion is not. These problems are severely compounded when addressing

sex between men due to the social taboo of homosexuality generally and discrimination against gay men in particular. (Hickson et al. 2000, 6)

Yet few have closely examined the ways in which gay male sexual subjectivities might feature kernels of resistance that pose formidable challenges to
traditional health promotion models. This issue raises vexing questions with
profound implications for our work with gay men. If resistance to health promotion is deeply rooted in the sexual subjectivities of a large portion of gay
men—and if this resistance is linked to our production of ourselves as
gender-nonconforming, sexual outlaws—will *any* forms of health promotion
serve to improve the health and wellness of gay men? Or should we set aside
(and defund) top-down health promotion efforts and move toward popular education, community organizing, and grassroots mobilization models that are
all too rarely supported in American public health today?

8

Toward a Radical Rethinking of Education, Schooling, and Sexuality

I recently was invited to return to the K–8 school where I taught when I was in my twenties. This small private school was celebrating its thirty-fifth anniversary by hosting a panel focused on the history and current practice of progressive education. I was fortunate to be included on this panel with Mary Hill, a longtime leader in the field from the Cambridge, Massachusetts, private progressive school crowd; and Alfie Kohn, the noted author and advocate for humane education for all kids. I felt honored to be included to share my thinking, as in the audience were noted progressive educators who had mentored me at the school more than two decades ago, including Sara and Bill Hull, Charlie Rathbone, and Jorie Hunken. The following day I was invited to visit the school and talk with the faculty about a number of issues and to participate in the weekly all-school meeting, where kids from all grades share projects, stories, and songs with their schoolmates.

This was no ordinary school meeting. It was the school's annual "lesbian and gay pride" school meeting, where classes make special presentations on their studies of gay history, culture, and politics. As an openly gay teacher hired by this daring and principled school twenty-five years earlier, I was thought to carry a bit of history that the faculty wanted me to impart.

Three women who had been eleven-, twelve-, and thirteen-year-old students in my first class at the school joined me at the meeting and contributed to our collective presentation of this chapter in the school's history. Now in their late thirties, two of them were working as teachers at the school, and the third had just published her first novel. When I was invited to give a brief presentation about gay issues in our era at the school, I imagined that the current kids would find more useful the perspective of the school's former students, who had dealt with the surprising news that their teacher was gay during a time when such events were not common; in other words, having an aging former teacher tell his story might be a big yawn.

As we settled into our seats in the school's gymnasium, I felt a mixture of joy at being with my former students, excitement at getting reacquainted with the school, and anticipation with the upcoming assembly. I am not sure what I imagined, but I never expected the meeting to begin with the kindergarten, first-, and second-grade classes' "Gay Pride Parade," consisting of scooters and tricycles decked out like gay day floats, signs saying "Gay is OK," and balloons and Mardi Gras beads tossed to the audience. A huge rainbow flag hung behind the stage as the 1970s disco anthem "We Are Family" came over the sound system. Parents, teachers, and students all seemed to share in this festival of lesbian and gay pride at their school.

This celebratory opening was followed by an earnest teacher or two, proclaiming how great the school was for embracing this particular cause, as well as some presentations by middle school students focused on the persecution of gays in the Holocaust. A separate team of students shared their observations of a meeting they had with members of a gay–straight alliance from the local public high school. I was especially struck with one ten-year-old girl's presentation about a female-to-male transgender high school student who had shifted his identity from that of a lesbian to a gay male. Trans issues making an appearance at my former school! This world is changing.

I was called to the stage by an old friend who worked as the school nurse; she highlighted the narrative I had helped to create for myself a quarter-century ago. I was heralded as a teacher who had come out in a job in another school and had been fired, only to be welcomed in and warmly embraced by this progressive school. I mumbled a few awkward words, and then my three students shared their recollections of being a kid in the 1970s when their teacher popped out of the closet. I was especially struck by Sarah's comments; she identifies as a bisexual, and she discussed how this early experience with queerdom made her own path somewhat easier.

Yet as I sat in the gymnasium and enjoyed the school's gay pride festivities, I realized that I saw before me what some might see as the culmination of a quarter-century of our collective work addressing gay issues in schools. I was heartened that this school had welcomed dozens of openly lesbian and gay teachers and parents into its fold since my own days as a teacher and by the fact that students now learned about gay issues as part of their classroom curriculum. The school has clearly brought about meaningful change in a relatively short period.

At the same time, I found myself reflecting on the discourse surrounding gay issues at the school and the powerful narrative of queers as victims or survivors that threaded through the celebration. What did these children really know about gay people? What could they know? How would this school cope with an openly gay fourth grader? Did an embracing of lesbians and gay men by the school make the children and teachers more open to supporting gender-nonconforming children, explicit sex education, and the full empowerment of kids?

I could not answer these questions after spending only a day or two at the school. But I was left thinking about the ways liberal people of privilege—including myself—embrace the other. Do we use the victim narrative to stir up empathy, with the expectation that empathy will lead one to supporting human rights for a formerly despised population? What are the politics behind utilizing the martyr–target–victim paradigm to move toward social acceptance of any population? (Rofes 2004). Do we do children a disservice by teaching them about Matthew Shepard and gays killed in the Holocaust, rather than inculcating them into the belief that all people deserve basic human rights, even those with whom we do not empathize—even those with who we disagree or find not worthy of our empathy?

THE PITFALLS OF LIBERAL APPROACHES

Liberal approaches to schooling, sexuality, and gender have resulted in significant changes within education throughout the United States, many of them important to the everyday lives of real people. Teachers have successfully won the right to be openly gay, lesbian, or bisexual in most parts of the country. Gay–straight alliances now supplement the drama club and the girls' softball team as sites where queers might find one another. Student newspapers and mainstream journalism alike have increasingly included coverage of gay issues in schools—ranging from queers attending proms to homophobic bullying to debates about the Boy Scouts.

Yet are these changes any different than the changes in American public education for African Americans in the fifty years since *Brown vs. Board of Education*, the Supreme Court decision heralded as promising every black child a quality education? In fact, have repeated attempts at desegregation, multicultural education, Title I funding, and Black History Month truly improved the educational achievement and transformed the life chances of African American children throughout the nation?

Although these changes have had their impact, I argue that for schools to fully eradicate racism or homophobia and become authentic sites of radical transformation for the culture, fundamental alterations must be made in the ways we conceptualize, organize, and deliver education. Furthermore, liberal approaches to gay issues in schools might have stripped a level of camouflage off many queer students without providing them with the resources and support to make real change in their schools. Liberal approaches might open more questions than they answer: In what ways do queer youth make meaning of the martyr–target–victim discourse, and what is its ultimate effect on their understandings of themselves? Do gender-normed, desexed lesbian and gay teachers promote social acceptance for those who are gender normed and desexed while creating hostility toward the outlaw queers? Who is ultimately served by the failure of liberal approaches to confront core issues of power in schools and between adults, youth, and children? Have our efforts of the past quarter-century done anything to ensure that young people have greater autonomy and authority in the world, freed them from the constraints of their families, or provided them with the kind of empowerment to step beyond the usual boundaries of social propriety?

If our interests are in a deep and fundamental transformation of the conditions that have created schools as sites of replication for the power imbalances and the cultural hierarchies of the status quo, our work on gay issues in schools might begin to confront some of the core issues driving the current organization of schooling:

- We must examine the ways colonizing approaches to childhood and adolescence have inspired the current organization of schools, classrooms, and pedagogy, and we must create new processes for organizing learning that are rooted in contemporary, emancipatory constructs. This involves a fundamental rethinking toward many of the theories and practices held dear, even by progressive educators: developmentalism, forms of classroom management, forced schooling.
- Rethinking the ways in which we organize teacher identity seems central to interrupting power imbalances that function to oppress and control children and youth. Shifting from teacher as source of wisdom to teacher as facilitator of learning seems key, as well as deconstructing teacher functions such as "role model" and "disciplinarian." Welcoming into teaching a range of people who do not adhere to narrow norms in the ways they organize their gender and sexuality seems especially critical to ending oppressive regimes of power that reproduce the status quo.
- If schools are about preparing people to become activist citizens in a democracy, then schools must be reorganized as models of authentic participatory democracy. This means that children and adolescents must have a voice and a vote on all the central matters involving curriculum, pedagogy, school organization, and the power dynamics circulating among groups of peers. This might be phased in from kindergarten forward, but by the time children reach middle school, they should be full

and active participants in the central issues involved in their lives in schools.

At the very least, it is time for queer community organizations to take a serious and thoughtful look on policy matters affecting public education in the United States, much more thoughtful than their efforts of the past few decades. We can no longer be content with handling the "LGBT piece" of this puzzle as if it were an additive feature. Instead, we must come to understand how the radical reforms needed to transform the educational experiences of queer and gender-nonconforming youth are precisely those reforms that might best benefit all marginalized populations—and privileged populations as well. Rather than turn another generation of youth over to policymakers who have repeatedly failed poor, minority, and queer youth, we need to draw together cutting-edge thinkers in these communities and create a new vision for remaking public education that places those currently marginalized at the center of our agenda.

A QUEER APPROACH TO EDUCATION POLICY ISSUES

I recently attended a foundation-funded meeting in Minneapolis of about thirty researchers, academics, and advocates who work on gay issues in schools throughout the United States. All participants had been sent a literature review, with some initial policy positions to consider as part of our discussions. As I expected, the literature review focused on LGBT youth and included dozens of pages reviewing the literature focused on the martyr–target–victim experience of queer youth. About a quarter-page of the review focused on "asset-based approaches" and "resiliency" among queer youth. I could hardly fault the diligent author; she had simply captured—in a powerful way—the stranglehold exerted by the victimization worldview on our knowledge of this population.

Also not unexpectedly, the policy section on "school choice" offered a succinct and simpleminded statement of the benefits and problems of school choice but failed to even suggest that queer youth in particular might be one population that would be especially benefited by choice. Instead, as has occurred throughout the past decade, queer groups working on issues related to education cede expertise on school choice matters primarily to the unions, who have taken both overt and covert positions against specific forms of school choice. This same dynamic occurred here despite the fact that the literature review had over a dozen examples of queer youth utilizing school choice mechanisms as tactics to maximize safety.

Though I was not surprised by the text, I was eager to see where the discussion would lead. On the opening night, our dinner speaker was Jamie Nabozny, who as a young man had sued his rural Wisconsin school district for not taking sufficient steps to protect him from a range of violations during his junior high and high school years. Nabozny had won a settlement of nearly $1 million and had become a symbol to the queer youth movement of fighting back. In fact, in the aftermath of his case, the Clinton-era Department of Education sent an advisory memo to all districts in the country, apprising them of the court decision and encouraging them to understand that antigay harassment was likely to be prosecuted in as powerful ways as general sexual harassment.

Nabozny told his story, and a powerful one it is. He spoke graphically about the verbal, physical, and sexual abuse and about the various ways he sought help and tried to cope. It was a horrific narrative. As the account unfolded, it became clear to me that the school-choice measures available in Minnesota and Wisconsin had served as lifeboats to this young man. His first move was to a local K–8 Catholic school, which his working-class farming family could barely find a way to afford. Then he took advantage of interdistrict choice and fled to a district closer to the Twin Cities, where he thought he would find more progressive educators. He tried to get into one of the nation's first charter schools but ultimately had to return to his original district, where the harassment escalated, culminating in his assault and rape in the boys' bathroom.

The story held the audience mesmerized, and they offered huge applause when Nabozny finished his tale. A few questions followed. Finally, there was a break in the questions, and I raised my hand and asked the speaker to share his perspective on policy questions related to school choice. He clearly hesitated before answering but then launched into a spirited defense of school choice, including vouchers. Highlighting his own experience and those of friends and colleagues who had been similarly abused in public school settings, he spoke of school choice as a safety net that allowed young people who were forced to be in public school to strategically move to safer spaces. Despite our host organization's lukewarm feelings toward school choice, Nabozny's talk was a ringing endorsement for choice mechanisms as a lifeline for persecuted and terrorized young people.

I highlight this example not to suggest that queer activists endorse vouchers or immerse themselves deeply into the political battles surrounding school choice but to show how complex educational issues are and how critically important these matters are to our community. Clearly, our work as educators, policymakers, and activists is cut out for us. After so much time pushing for incremental change in the field of education, is it any wonder the status quo remains largely entrenched?

This book does not ask us to regard all our earlier work on LGBT issues in education as misguided. It does ask us to consider those efforts to be a first-stage response with all of the strengths and weaknesses, mistakes and successes of the first generation of efforts in any policy area. And it insists that we look critically at the strategies we have chosen, the tactics we have used, and the shifting contexts in which we do this work as we create a second-stage of strategic approaches.

Most of all, it demands that we take a fearless look at the downside of the liberal love affair with slow and incremental change and consider radical approaches that strike at the root causes of oppression, marginalization, and injustice in our schools and other public institutions.

Appendix: School of Education Documents

Bank Street Graduate School of Education
  _ *Application for Admission to the Graduate School*
  _ *Catalogue, 1994–1996*

Boston University
  _ *School of Education, 1994/1995, Graduate Programs*

Harvard University
  _ *Application for Admission*
  _ *School of Education, 1993–1994, Bulletin*

Ohio State University
  _ *Graduate Programs, College of Education*
  _ *Graduate School Admission Application*
  _ *Graduate Studies in Educational Administration*
  _ *School Psychology Programs*

Stanford University
  _ *Courses, Degrees, and Information, 1994–95*
  _ *School of Education Information Bulletin, 1994–1995*

Teachers College, Columbia University
  _ *1994/1995 Bulletin*
  _ *Application for Admission*
  _ *Application for Residence Halls*
  _ *Application for Student Aid*

University of Buffalo, State University of New York
_ *Graduate School of Education, 1993–1996, Catalog*

University of California at Berkeley
_ *General Catalog 1994–1995*
_ *Graduate School of Education, 1994–1995, Announcement and Application*

University of California at Los Angeles
_ *Application for Admission, Fall Quarter 1995*
_ *Graduate School of Education, 1993–1994, Announcement*
_ *Graduate School of Education and Information Studies, 1994–1995, Faculty Roster*

University of Chicago
_ *Graduate Studies in Education, 1994–1995*
_ *Graduate Application for Admission and Aid*

University of Massachusetts at Amherst
_ *1994/1995, Graduate Student Bulletin*
_ *Graduate School Application*

University of Michigan
_ *Educational Studies Application Checklist*
_ *Peace Corps Fellows/USA Program brochure*
_ *School of Education Graduate Programs, Bulletin 24, no. 2 (July 27, 1994)*

University of North Carolina at Chapel Hill
_ *Curriculum and Instruction, Ed.D.*
_ *Curriculum and Instruction, Ph.D.*
_ *Educational Leadership, Ed.D.*
_ *Educational Organization and Policy Studies, Ph.D.*
_ *Educational Psychology, Ph.D.*
_ *School Psychology, Ph.D.*
_ *Shaping Your Future in Education*
_ *Social Foundations, Ph.D.*
_ *Special Education, Ph.D.*

University of Southern California
  _ *Application for Graduate Admission, 1995–1996*
  _ *Policy and Organization Ph.D. Program, Program Description*
  _ *School of Education, Bulletin, 1994–1995*

University of Wisconsin at Madison
  _ *Department of Educational Policy Studies Graduate Handbook*
  _ *Faculty Profiles in Educational Psychology*
  _ *Graduate Training in Educational Psychology*
  _ *Rehabilitation Counseling Master's Degree Program*
  _ *School of Education Bulletin, 1993–1995*
  _ *Special Education M.S./M.A. Degree Program*

Vanderbilt University
  _ *The Graduate School: Application and Guide to Admission*

Wheelock College
  _ *Graduate Catalogue, 1994–1995*

References

Abelove, H., R. Ohmann, and C. B. Potter. 1994. Introduction. *Radical Teacher* 45 (2).

Adams, P., L. Berg, N. Berger, M. Duane, A. S. Neill, and R. Ollendorff. 1971. *Children's rights: Toward the liberation of the child*. New York: Praeger.

AIDS Council of New South Wales. 2000. *Give a fuck*. Sydney, Australia: Author.

Albrecht, L. 1993. Tenured, out, and still composed. Paper presented at the annual meeting of the Conference on College Composition and Communications, San Diego, Calif., March 31–April 3.

Alden, J. 1992. *A boy's best friend*. Boston: Alyson Wonderland.

Alderson, 1994. Children's rights. In *Children's childhoods observed and experienced*, ed. B. Mayall. London: Falmer.

Alinsky, S. 1971. *Rules for radicals: A pragmatic primer for realistic radicals*. New York: Vintage Books.

American Educational Research Association. 1995. Annual meeting program, April 18–22. San Francisco, Calif.: Author.

Andriette, B. 1983. Liberation: Participation, not passivity. *NAMBLA Journal* 6:6–7.

———. 1992. Intergenerational sex: Consent isn't the problem. *Empathy* 3 (1): 100–102.

Anthony, E. J., and B. Cohler, eds. 1987. *The invulnerable child*. New York: Guilford.

Archer, B. 1999. *The end of gay (and the death of heterosexuality)*. Toronto: Doubleday.

Aries, 1965. *Centuries of childhood: A social history of family life*. New York: Random House.

Atlas, R., and D. Pepler. 1998. Observations of bullying in the classroom. *Journal of Educational Research* 92 (2): 86–99.

Austin, J., and M. N. Willard. 1998a. *Generations of youth: Youth cultures and history in twentieth-century America*. New York: New York University Press.

———. 1998b. Introduction: Angels of history, demons of culture. In *Generations of youth: Youth cultures and history in twentieth-century America.* New York: New York University Press.

Bakan, D. 1976. Adolescence in America: From idea to social fact. In *Rethinking childhood: Perspectives on development and society,* ed. A. Skolnick. Boston: Little, Brown.

Bank Street College. 1994–1996. *Graduate School of Education catalogue.* New York: Author.

Barale, M. E. 1994. The romance of class and queers: Academic erotic zones. In *Tilting the tower: Lesbians teaching queer subjects,* ed. L. Garber, 16–24. New York: Routledge.

Bass, E., and K. Kaufman. 1996. *Free your mind. The book for gay, lesbian, and bisexual youth—and their allies.* New York: HarperCollins.

Bawer, B. 1995. Family values key to gay rights. *San Francisco Sentinel,* January 25, 13.

Beane, A. 1999. *The bully free classroom: Over 100 tips and strategies for teachers K–8.* Minneapolis, Minn.: Free Spirit Publishing.

Besner, J., and C. Spungin. 1995. *Gay and lesbian students: Understanding their needs.* Washington, D.C.: Taylor and Francis.

Bias policy widened to include gay students. 1994. *New York Times,* June 23.

Blumenfeld, W. 1995a. "Gay/straight" alliances: Transforming pain to pride. In *The gay teen: Educational practice and theory for lesbian, gay, and bisexual adolescents,* ed. G. Unks, 211–24. New York: Routledge.

———. 1995b. Recovering the past: A gay, lesbian, and bisexual history. Slide presentation, Northampton, Mass.

———. 1996. History/hysteria: Parallel representations of Jews and gays, lesbians, and bisexuals. In *Queer studies: A lesbian, gay, bisexual, and transgender anthology,* ed. B. Beemyn and M. Eliason. New York: New York University Press.

Blumstein, P., and P. Schwartz. 1993. *American couples: Money, work, sex.* New York: William Morris.

Boldt, G. 1997. Sexist and heterosexist responses to gender bending. In *Making a place for pleasure in early childhood education,* ed. J. Tobin, 188–213. New Haven, Conn.: Yale University Press.

Boston University School of Education. 1994–1995. *Graduate programs.*

Bourdieu, P. 1982. *The logic of practice.* Palo Alto, Calif.: Stanford University Press.

———. 1984. *Distinction: A social critique of the judgment of taste.* Cambridge, Mass.: Harvard University Press.

Bradley, A. 1995. Holmes group urges overhaul of ed. schools. *Education Week,* February 1, 1.

Brake, M. 1980. *The sociology of youth culture and youth subcultures.* Boston: Routledge and Kegan Paul.

Brandenburg, J. B. 1997. *Confronting sexual harassment : What schools and colleges can do.* New York: Teachers College Press.

Brogan, J. 1995. Gay teens in literature. In *The gay teen: Educational practice and theory for lesbian, gay, and bisexual adolescents,* ed. G. Unks, 67–78. New York: Routledge.

Bronski, M., ed. 1996. *Flashpoint: Gay male sexual writing.* New York: Masquerade Books.

———. 1998. *The pleasure principle: Sex, backlash, and the struggle for gay freedom.* New York: St. Martin's.

Brookey, R. 2002. *Reinventing the male homosexual: The rhetoric and power of the gay gene.* Bloomington: University of Indiana Press.

Butler, J. 1993. *Bodies that matter: On the discursive limits of "sex."* New York: Routledge.

Cable, M. 1975. *The little darlings: A history of child rearing in America.* New York: Charles Scribner's Sons.

Cage, M. C. 1994. A course on homosexuality. *Chronicle of Higher Education,* December 14, A19.

Califia, P. 1994. *Public sex: The culture of radical sex.* San Francisco: Cleis.

Calluori, R. A. 1985. The kids are alright: New wave subcultural theory. *Social Text* 12 (Fall): 43–53.

Campbell, K. 1994a. Anti-gay language struck from ed. bill. *Washington Blade,* September 23, 1.

———. 1994b. High school student drops out over harassment. *Washington Blade,* June 10, 25.

Campbell, K., and L. Chibbaro Jr. 1995. Youth suicide, AIDS cure bill's back. *Washington Blade,* February 10, 20.

Carnes, N. A. 1995. Lapdog mentality [letter to the editor]. *Washington Blade,* March 10, 43.

Casper, V., H. Cuffaro, S. Schults, J. Silin, and E. Wickens. 1996. Toward a most thorough understanding of the world: Sexual orientation and early childhood education. *Harvard Educational Review* 66 (2): 271–93.

Casper, V., S. Schultz, and E. Wickens. 1992. Breaking the silences: Lesbian and gay parents and the schools. *Teacher College Record* 94 (1): 109–37.

Catholic school students irked by sex ed. class. 1995. *Washington Blade,* March 24, 16.

Chapkis, W. 1994. Explicit instruction: Talking sex in the classroom. In *Tilting the tower: Lesbians teaching queer subjects,* ed. L. Garber, 11–15. New York: Routledge.

Chauncey, G. 1993. The postwar sex crime panic. In *True stories from the American past,* ed. W. Graebner, 160–78. New York: McGraw-Hill.

Chibbaro, L., Jr. 1995. Rhode Island's 1994 Teacher of the Year is gay. *Washington Blade,* March 24, 1.

City University of New York. 1994. *The CLAGS directory of lesbian and gay studies.* Center for Lesbian and Gay Studies.

Cleverley, J., and D. C. Phillips. 1986. *Visions of childhood: Iinfluential models from Locke to Spock.* New York: Teachers College Press.

Community forum: NAMBLA: Community or criminal? 1992. *San Francisco Bay Times,* January 30, 8–9.

Connell, R. W. 1989. Cool guys, swots, and wimps: The interplay of masculinity and education. *Oxford Review of Education* 15 (3): 291–303.

———. 1995. *Masculinities.* Berkeley: University of California Press.

Cote, J., and A. Allahar. 1996. *Generation on hold: Coming of age in the late twentieth century.* New York: New York University Press.

Coveney, P. 1976. The image of the child in English Literature. In *Rethinking childhood: Perspectives on development and society,* ed. A. Skolnick. Boston: Little, Brown.

Craig, W., and D. Pepler. 1997. Observations of bullying and victimization in the schoolyard. *Canadian Journal of School Psychology* 13 (2): 41–60.

Crompton, L. 1993. Gay and lesbian students, ROTC, and the new rules. *Academe* 79 (5): 8–12.

Cuban, L., ed. 1971. *Youth as a minority: An anatomy of students' rights.* Washington, D.C.: National Council for the Social Studies.

———. 1995. *How teachers taught: Constancy and change in American classrooms.* New York: Teachers College Press.

Dangerous Bedfellows. 1996. Introduction. In *Policing public sex,* ed. Dangerous Bedfellows. Boston: South End Press.

DeMause, L., ed. 1974. *The history of childhood.* New York: Psychohistory Press.

D'Emilio, J., and E. Freedman. 1988. *Intimate matters: A history of sexuality in America.* New York: Harper and Row.

Diamond, J. 1995. Gingrich accuses gays of "recruitment." *San Francisco Frontiers,* March 16, 5.

Dines, G., R. Jensen, and A. Russo. 1998. *Pornography: The production and consumption of inequality.* New York: Routledge.

Dizard, J., and H. Gadlin. 1990. *The minimal family.* Amherst: University of Massachusetts Press.

Donahue, W., ed. 1998. *Sexual harassment: Theory, research, and treatment.* Boston: Allyn and Bacon.

Due, L. 1995. *Joining the tribe: Growing up gay and lesbian in the '90s.* New York: Doubleday.

Dworkin, A. 1988. *Letters from a war zone.* London: Secker and Warburg.

Eckert, 1989. *Jocks and burnouts: Social categories and identity in the high school.* New York: Teachers College Press.

Elkind, D. 1981. *The hurried child: Growing up too fast, too soon.* Reading, Mass.: Addison-Wesley.

Ellis, H. 1942. *Studies in the psychology of sex.* New York: Random House.

Elovich, R. 1999. Beyond condoms. *Poz,* June, 81–91.

Epstein, D. 1994. *Challenging lesbian and gay inequalities in education.* Buckingham, Eng.: Open University Press.

———. 1998. Real boys don't work: "Underachievement," masculinity and the harassment of "sissies." In *Failing boys? Issues in gender and achievement,* ed. D. Epstein, J. Elwood, V. Hey, and J. Maw. Buckingham, Eng.: Open University Press.

Epstein, D., Elwood, J., Hey, V. and Maw, J. 1998a. *Failing boys? Issues in gender and achievement.* Buckingham, Eng.: Open University Press.

———, eds. 1998b. Schoolboy frictions: Feminism and "failing" boys. In *Failing boys? Issues in gender and achievement,* ed. D. Epstein, J. Elwood, V. Hey, and J. Maw. Buckingham, Eng.: Open University Press.

Epstein, D., and R. Johnson. 1998. *Schooling sexualities*. Buckingham, Eng.: Open University Press.

Fausto-Sterling, A. 2000. *Sexing the body: Gender politics and the construction of sexuality*. New York: Basic Books.

Fine, M. 1988. Sexuality, schooling, and adolescent females: The missing discourse of desire. *Harvard Educational Review* 58 (1): 49.

———. 1991. *Framing dropouts: Notes on the politics of an urban public high school*. Albany: State University of New York Press.

Finkelstein, B. 1985. Casting networks of good influence: The reconstruction of childhood in the United States, 1790–1870. In *American childhood: A research guide and historical handbook*, ed. J. Hawes and N. R. Hiner. Westport, Conn.: Greenwood Press.

Firestone, S. 1970. *The dialectic of sex*. New York: William Morrow.

Flint, T. 1994, May 13. Fundamentalists take aim at equal education for gay/lesbian students. *Seattle Gay News*, 11.

Fordham, S. 1996. *Blacked out: Dilemmas of race, identity, and success at Capital High*. Chicago: University of Chicago Press.

Foucault, M. 1977. *Discipline and punish: The birth of the prison*. New York: Random House.

———. 1978. *The history of sexuality*. Vol. 1, *An introduction*. New York: Pantheon.

Fraser, M. W., ed. 1997. *Risk and resilience in childhood: An ecological perspective*. Washington, D.C.: NASW Press.

Freedman, E. 1989. "Uncontrolled desires": The response to the sexual psychopath, 1920–1960. In *Passion and power: Sexuality in history*, 199–240. Philadelphia: Temple University Press.

Freiberg, P. 1995. Drama in Des Moines. *Washington Blade*, January 27, 16.

Freire, P. 1970. *Pedagogy of the oppressed*. New York: Continuum.

Frye, M. 1983. *The politics of reality*. Freedom, Calif.: Crossing Press.

Gallagher, J. 1991. Hypothalamus study and coverage of it attracts many barbs. *Advocate*, October 8, 14–15.

Gallop, J. 1988. *Thinking through the body*. New York: Columbia University Press.

———. 1997. *Feminist accused of sexual harassment*. Durham, N.C.: Duke University Press.

Gallup, G. 1987. Homosexuality: Backlash against gays appears to be leveling off. *Gallup Report* 258 (March): 12.

Gay Men Fighting AIDS. 2001. *Bareback* campaign. London.

———. 2002. *Enjoy fucking?* campaign. London.

Glaser, C. 1993. The religious right: Infiltrating our public schools. *Sojourner: The Women's Forum* (Boston), December, 15.

Glover, D., N. Cartwright, and D. Gleeson. 1998. *Towards bully-free schools: Interventions in action*. Buckingham, Eng.: Open University Press.

Gordon, L. 1988. *Heroes of their own lives: The politics and history of family violence*. New York: Viking.

Green, H., and N. Ordover. 1994. Out of these silences: Voicing race, gender, and sexuality in ethnic studies. *Radical Teacher* 45 (2): 42–46.

Greenberg, D. 1990. *The construction of homosexuality.* Chicago: University of Chicago Press.

Greene, B. 1999. On locating homosexuality in American culture. Paper presented at Beyond AIDS: Launching a Multi-issue, Multicultural Gay Men's Health Movement, Boulder County AIDS Project, Boulder, Colo.

Griffin, C. 1993. *Representations of youth: The study of youth and adolescence in Britain and America.* Cambridge, Mass.: Polity Press.

Griffin, K. 1994. Helms amendments come up for negotiation. *Bay Area Reporter* (San Francisco), October 19.

Gross, B., and R. Gross, eds. 1977. *The children's rights movement: Overcoming the oppression of young people.* New York: Anchor Books.

Gross, J. 1994. In school. *New York Times*, June 27, B8.

Hale, K., and S. Donahue. 1997. Gay, lesbian, and bisexual students at risk: Nuggets—news, notes, and findings from ADAP research and planning unit. Burlington, Vt.: Vermont Department of Health, Office of Alcohol and Drug Abuse Programs.

Halperin, D. 1990. *One hundred years of homosexuality.* New York: Routledge.

Harachi, T., R. Catalano, and J. D. Hawkins. 1999. United States. In *The nature of school bullying: A cross-national perspective,* ed. P. K. Smith, Y. Morita, J. Junger-Tas, D. Olweus, R. Catalano, and P. Slee. New York: Routledge.

Harbeck, K., ed. 1992. *Coming out of the classroom closet: Gay and lesbian students, teachers, and curricula.* Binghamton, N.Y.: Haworth Press.

Hendrick, H. 1990. Constructions and reconstructions of British childhood: An interpretative survey, 1800 to the present. In *Constructing and reconstructing childhood: Contemporary issues in the sociological study of childhood,* ed. A. James and A. Prout. New York: Falmer.

Herdt, G., and A. Boxer. 1993. *Children of horizons: How gay and lesbian teens are leading a new way out of the closet.* Boston: Beacon Press.

Heron, A., ed. 1993. *One teenager in 10: Writings by gay and lesbian youth.* Boston: Alyson Publications.

Heron, A., and M. Maran. 1991. *How would you feel if your dad was gay?* Boston: Alyson Wonderland.

Hickson, F. 2000. *Making it count: A collaborative planning framework to reduce the incidence of HIV infection during sex between men.* London: Sigma Research.

High school council passes a gay ban on leaders. 1993. *New York Times*, May 16.

Hodgdon, P. 1995a. E. J. Byington, 17, dies of suicide. *Bay Area Reporter* (San Francisco), February 2, 19.

———. 1995b. Dornan's bigotry. *Bay Guardian* (San Francisco), March 8, 11.

Holland, D. C., and M. A. Eisenhart. 1990. *Educated in romance: Women, achievement, and college culture.* Chicago: University of Chicago Press.

Holt, J. C. 1975. *Escape from childhood: The needs and rights of children.* Harmondsworth, Eng.: Penguin.

hooks, b. 1994. *Teaching to transgress: Education as the practice of freedom.* New York: Routledge.

Horton, H., and P. Freire. 1990. *We make the road by walking: Conversations on education and social change.* Philadelphia: Temple University Press.

In 1994, *Daddy's Roommate* was most challenged. 1995. *Washington Blade*, March 17, 22.

James, A., and A. Prout, eds. 1990. *Constructing and reconstructing childhood: Contemporary issues in the sociological study of childhood.* New York: Falmer.

Jencks, C. 1982. *The sociology of childhood.* London: Batsford.

Jennings, K., ed. 1994a. *Becoming visible: A reader in gay and lesbian history for high school and college students.* Boston: Alyson Publications.

———, ed. 1994b. *One teacher in 10: Gay and lesbian educators tell their stories.* Boston: Alyson.

Jew, C. L., and K. E. Green. 1998. Effects of risk factors on adolescents' resiliency and coping. *Psychological Reports* 82:675–78.

Jew, C., K. Green, J. Millard, and M. Posillico. 1999. *Resiliency: An examination of related factors in a sample of students from an urban high school and a residential child care facility.* Paper presented at the American Educational Research Association Annual Meeting, Montreal, April.

Johnson-Calvo, S. 1991. *A beach party with Alexis: A coloring book.* Boston: Alyson Publications.

Katz, J. 1983. *Gay/lesbian almanac.* New York: Harper and Row.

———. 1990. The invention of heterosexuality. *Socialist Review* 20 (1): 7–34.

Katznelson, I., and M. Weir. 1985. *Schooling for all: Class, race, and the decline of the democratic ideal.* New York: Basic Books.

Keen, L., and L. Chibbaro. 1998. Starr outing adultery: What America does and doesn't want to know. *New York Blade News*, September 18, 12.

Keogh, P. 2001. *How to be a healthy homosexual: A study of CHAPS HIV health promotion with gay men.* London: Sigma Research.

Kett, J. 1977. *Rites of passage: Adolescence in America: 1790 to the present.* New York: Basic Books.

Khayatt, D. 1994. Surviving school as a lesbian student. *Gender and Education* 6 (1): 59.

Khayatt, M. 1992. *Lesbian teachers: An invisible presence.* Albany: State University of New York Press.

Kincaid, J. 1992. *Child-loving: The erotic child and Victorian culture.* New York: Routledge.

———. 1998. *Erotic innocence: The culture of child molesting.* Durham, N.C.: Duke University Press.

King, J. 1998. *Uncommon caring: Learning from men who teach young children.* New York: Teachers College Press.

Kissen, R. 1993. *Voices from the glass closet: Lesbian and gay teachers talk about their lives.* Paper presented at the annual meeting of the American Educational Research Association, Atlanta, Ga., April.

———. 1996. *The last closet: The real lives of lesbian and gay teachers.* Portsmouth, N.H.: Heinemann.

Kitzinger, C. 1987. *Social construction of lesbianism.* Thousand Oaks, Calif.: Sage.

Kitzinger, J. 1990. Who are you kidding? Children, power, and the struggle against sexual abuse. In *Constructing and reconstructing childhood: Contemporary issues in the sociological study of childhood,* ed. A. James and A. Prout. New York: Falmer.

Klinger, A. 1994. Moving the pink agenda into the ivory tower: The "Berkeley Guide" to institutionalizing lesbian, gay, and bisexual studies. In *Tilting the tower: Lesbians teaching queer subjects,* ed. L. Garber, 186–97. New York: Routledge.

Kohlberg, L. 1981. *The philosophy of moral development.* San Francisco: Harper and Row.

Kourany, R. E. 1987. Suicide among homosexual adolescents. *Journal of Homosexuality* 13:111–17.

Krafft-Ebing, R. von. 1899. *Psychopathia sexualis.* London: F. A. Davis.

Kumashiro, K. 2001. *Troubling intersections of race and sexuality: Queer students of color and anti-oppressive education.* Lanham, Md.: Rowman and Littlefield.

Langford, P. 1995. *Approaches to the development of moral reasoning.* Mahwah, N.J.: Lawrence Erlbaum.

Lansdown, G. 1994. Researching children's rights to integrity. In *Children's childhoods observed and experienced,* ed. B. Mayall. London: Falmer.

Larkin, J. 1994. *Sexual harassment: High school girls speak out.* New York: Second Story Press.

LaSalle, L. A. 1992. Exploring campus intolerance: A textual analysis of comments concerning lesbian, gay, and bisexual people. Paper presented at the annual meeting of the American Educational Research Association, San Francisco, Calif., April.

Lave, J., and E. Wenger. 1991. *Situated learning.* Cambridge: Cambridge University Press.

Lee, E., D. Menkart, and M. Okazawa-Rey, eds. 1997. *Beyond heroes and holidays: A practical guide to K-12 anti-racist, multicultural education staff development.* Washington, D.C.: Teaching for Change.

Lee, N., D. Murphy, and L. North. 1994. Sexuality, multicultural education, and the New York City public schools. *Radical Teacher* 45 (2): 12–16.

Lesbians, gays voted out of classroom. 1995. *San Francisco Sentinel,* March 22, 12.

Lesbian's sex talk triggers complaint. 1995. *Oakland Tribune,* March 8, A7.

Lewin, E. 1993. *Lesbian mothers: Accounts of gender in American culture.* Ithaca, N.Y.: Cornell University Press.

Lipkin, A. 1995. The case for a gay and lesbian curriculum. In *The gay teen: Educational practice and theory for lesbian, gay, and bisexual adolescents,* ed. G. Unks, 31–52. New York: Routledge.

Lopez, G., and N. Chism. 1993. Classroom concerns of gay and lesbian students: The invisible minority. *College Teaching* 41 (3): 99.

Lortie, D. 1975. *Schoolteacher: A sociological study.* Chicago: University of Chicago Press.

Luboff, G. 1992. Making choices: Determining the need to be out. Paper presented at the annual meeting of the Conference on College Composition and Communication, Cincinnati, Ohio, March.

Luker, K. 1996. *Dubious conceptions: The politics of teenage pregnancy.* Cambridge, Mass.: Harvard University Press.

Mac an Ghaill, M. 1994. *The making of men.* Buckingham, Eng.: Open University Press.

Mahony, P. 1998. Girls will be girls and boys will be first. In *Failing boys?: Issues in gender and achievement,* ed. D. Epstein, J. Elwood, V. Hey, and J. Maw. Buckingham, Eng.: Open University Press.

Mangan, K. S. 1995. Conservative students challenge support for campus gay organizations. *Chronicle of Higher Education,* January 27, A38.

Marriage rate in U.S. drops to record low: Far fewer spouses say they're "very happy." 1999. *San Francisco Chronicle,* July 2, 1.

Marshall, D., K. Kaplan, and J. Greenman. 1995. *The PERSON organizing manual: Public education regarding sexual orientation nationally.* Oakland, Calif.: PERSON Project.

Mayall, B., ed. 1994. *Children's childhoods observed and experienced.* London: Falmer.

McCready, L. 2001. When fitting in isn't an option, or, why black queer males at a California high school stay away from Project 10. In *Troubling intersections of race and sexuality: Queer students of color and anti-oppressive education,* ed. K. Kumashiro. Lanham, Md.: Rowman and Littlefield.

McDermott, R. 1987. Achieving school failure: An anthropological approach to literacy and social stratification. In *Education and cultural process: Anthropological approaches,* ed. G. Spindler, 2nd ed., 82–118. Prospect Heights, Ill.: Waveland.

McLaren, P. 1995. *Critical pedagogy and predatory culture.* New York: Routledge.

McMillen, J. C. 1999. Better for it: How people benefit from adversity. *Social Work* 44 (5): 455–67.

McRobbie, A. 1978. Working-class girls and the culture of femininity. In *Women take issue,* ed. Women's Studies Group, Centre for Contemporary Cultural Studies. London: Hutchinson.

McWilliam, E., and A. Jones. 1996. Eros and pedagogical bodies: The state of (non)affairs. In *Pedagogy, technology, and the body,* ed. E. McWilliam and P. Taylor, 127–36. New York: Peter Lang.

Mintz, S., and S. Kellogg. 1988. *Domestic revolutions: A social history of American family life.* New York: Free Press.

Mission statement. 1993. Massachusetts Safe Schools Program for Gay and Lesbian Students.

Moll, A. 1931. *Perversions of the sex instinct.* New York: Julian Press.

Monteiro, K., and V. Fuqua. 1995. African-American gay youth: One form of manhood. In *The gay teen: Educational practice and theory for lesbian, gay, and bisexual adolescents,* ed. G. Unks, 159–88. New York: Routledge.

Moran, J. 2000. *Teaching sex: The shaping of adolescence in the 20th century.* Cambridge, Mass.: Harvard University Press.

Muther, C. 1994. Hope for gay kids. *Bay Windows* (Boston), September 15–21, 1.

Nestle, J. 1998. *A fragile union: New and selected writings by Joan Nestle.* San Francisco: Cleis.

Newell, P. 1989. *Children are people too: The case against physical punishment.* London: Bedford Square Press.

Newman, L. 1989. *Heather has two mommies*. Boston: Alyson Wonderland.

———. 1991a. *Belinda's bouquet*. Boston: Alyson Wonderland.

———. 1991b. *Gloria goes to gay pride*. Boston: Alyson Wonderland.

Newman, M. 1995. An old debate being revived on curriculum. *New York Times*, February 14.

News item. 1995a. *San Francisco Bay Times*, March 9, 9.

News item. 1995b. *Advocate*, April 4, 10.

North American Man/Boy Love Association. 1992. Constitution and position papers. Boston, Massachusetts.

Note book. 1995. *Chronicle of Higher Education*, February 17, A37.

Obear, K. 1991. Homophobia. In *Beyond tolerance: Gays, lesbians, and bisexuals on campus*, ed. N. Evans and V. Wall, 39–66. Alexandria, Va.: American College Personnel Association.

O'Connor, A. 1995. Breaking the silence. Writing about gay, lesbian, and bisexual teenagers. In *The gay teen: Educational practice and theory for lesbian, gay, and bisexual adolescents*, ed. G. Unks, 13–16. New York: Routledge.

Owens, R. 1998. *Queer kids: The challenge and promise for lesbian, gay, and bisexual youth*. Binghamton, N.Y.: Haworth.

Palmer, P. 1996. Queer theory, homosexual teaching bodies, and an infecting pedagogy. In *Pedagogy, technology, and the body*, ed. E. McWilliam and P. Taylor, 79–88. New York: Peter Lang.

Patton, C. 1996. *Fatal advice: How safe-sex education went wrong*. Durham, N.C.: Duke University Press.

Pepler, D., W. Craig, S. Ziegler, and A. Charach. 1994. An evaluation of an anti-bullying intervention in Toronto Schools. *Canadian Journal of Community Mental Health* 13 (2): 95–110.

Peterfreund, N., and A. Cheadle. 1996. *Seattle Public Schools 1995 teen health risk survey*. Seattle, Wash.: Seattle Public Schools.

Pharr, S. 1996. *In the time of the right: Reflections on liberation*. Berkeley, Calif.: Chardon Press.

Phelan, A. 1997. Classroom management and the erasure of teacher desire. In *Making a place for pleasure in early childhood education*, ed. J. Tobin, 76–100. New Haven, Conn.: Yale University Press.

Pilkington, N. W., and A. R. D'Augelli. n.d. Victimization of lesbian, gay, and bisexual youth in community settings. McGill University, Department of Psychology; and Pennsylvania State University, Department of Human Development and Family Studies.

Platt, A. 1969. *The child savers: The invention of delinquency*. Chicago: University of Chicago Press.

Polite, V. and J. D. Davis. 1999. *African American males in school and society: Practices and policies for effective education*. New York: Teachers College Press.

Pollack, L. A. 1983. *Forgotten children: Parent-child relations from 1500–1900*. Cambridge: Cambridge University Press.

Pollack, R., and C. Schwartz. 1995. *The journey out: A guide for and about lesbian, gay, and bisexual teenagers*. New York: Viking.

Porter, Michael. 1998. *Kill them before they grow: The misdiagnosis of African American boys in America's classrooms.* Washington, D.C.: African American Images.

Portner, J. 1994. Districts adopting policies to protect gay students' rights. *Education Week,* October 5, 8.

Postman, N. 1982. *The disappearance of childhood.* New York: Dell.

Promoting diversity [editorial]. 1994. *Boston Globe,* June 30, 14.

Qvortrup, J., ed. 1993. *Childhood as a social phenomenon: Lessons from an international project.* Vienna: European Centre.

Reagon, B. 1983. Coalition politics: Turning the century. In *Home Girls: A black feminist anthology,* ed. B. Smith, 356–69. New York: Kitchen Table Press.

Reed, D. B. 1994. The sexualized context of American public high schools. Paper presented at the annual meeting of the American Educational Research Association, New Orleans, La., April.

Remafedi, G. 1991. Risk factors for attempted suicide in gay and bisexual youth. *Pediatrics* 87:869–75.

———. 1992. Demography of sexual orientation in adolescents. *Pediatrics* 89:714–21.

———, ed. 1994. *Death by denial: Studies of suicide in gay and lesbian teenagers.* Boston: Alyson Publications.

Rensenbrink, C. W. 1996. What difference does it make? The story of a lesbian teacher. *Harvard Educational Review* 66 (2): 257–70.

Research points toward a "gay" gene. 1993. *Wall Street Journal,* July 16, B1.

Rich, A. 1983. Compulsory heterosexuality and the lesbian existence. In *Powers of Desire,* ed. A. Snitow, 177–205. New York: Monthly Review Press.

Rofes, E., ed. 1981. *The kids' book of divorce: By, for, and about kids.* Lexington, Mass.: Lewis Publishing.

———. 1985. *Socrates, Plato, and guys like me: Confessions of a gay schoolteacher.* Boston: Alyson.

———. 1995a. AIDS, education, and democracy. Paper presented at the annual meeting of the American Educational Research Association, San Francisco, Calif., April.

———. 1995b. Making our schools safe for sissies. In *The gay teen: Educational practice and theory for lesbian, gay, and bisexual adolescents,* ed. G. Unks, 79–84. New York: Routledge.

———. 1996. *Reviving the tribe: Regenerating gay men's sexuality and culture in the ongoing epidemic.* Binghamton, N.Y.: Haworth.

———. 1998a. *Dry bones breathe: Gay men creating post-AIDS identities and cultures.* Binghamton, N.Y.: Haworth.

———. 1998b. Innocence, perversion, and Heather's two mommies. *Journal of Gay, Lesbian, and Bisexual Identity* 3 (1): 3–26.

———. 1999. What happens when the kids grow up? The long-term impact of an openly gay teacher on eight students' lives. In *Queering elementary education: Advancing the dialogue about sexualities and schooling,* ed. W. J. Letts and J. T. Sears, 83–96. Lanham, Md.: Rowman and Littlefield.

———. 2004. Martyr-target-victim: Interrogating narratives of persecution and suffering among queer youth. In. *Youth and sexuality: Pleasure, subversion, and insub-*

ordination in and out of schools, ed. M. Rasmussen, E. Rofes, and S. Talburt. New York: Palgrave.

Rubin, G. 1984. Thinking sex: Notes for a radical theory of the politics of sexuality. In *Pleasure and danger: Exploring female sexuality*, ed. C. Vance, 267–319. Boston: Routledge.

———. 1993. Thinking sex: Notes for a radical theory of the politics of sexuality. In *The lesbian and gay studies reader*, ed. H. Abelove, M. Barale, and D. Halperin, 3–44. New York: Routledge.

Ruenzel, D. 1994. Getting personal. *Teacher*, September, 25–29.

Russell, S., A. Driscoll, and N. Truong. 2002. Adolescent same-sex romantic attractions and relationships: Implications for substance use and abuse. *American Journal of Public Health* 92 (2): 198–202.

Ryan, C., and D. Futterman. 1998. *Lesbian and gay youth: Care and counseling*. New York: Columbia University Press.

Safe Schools Coaliton of Washington. 1999. *Eighty-three thousand youth: Selected findings of eight population-based studies as they pertain to anti-gay harassment and the safety and well-being of sexual minority students*. Seattle: Safe Schools Coalition.

Salisbury, J., and D. Jackson. 1996. *Challenging macho values: Practical ways of working with adolescent boys*. London: Falmer Press.

San Francisco AIDS Foundation. 2000a. "Barebacking": More than just a fuck. *Bay Area Reporter* (San Francisco), October 26.

San Francisco AIDS Foundation. 2000b. Gay sex ad campaign sparks community dialogue. *OUTReach: News you can use to fight HIV/AIDS*, December, 1.

Savin-Williams, R. 1999. ". . . And then I became gay": Young men's stories. New York: Routledge.

———. 2001. *Mom, dad, I'm gay: How families negotiate coming out*. Washington, D.C.: American Psychological Association.

Scarce, M. 1997. *Male on male rape: The hidden toll of stigma and shame*. New York: Insight Books.

———. 1999a. *Smearing the queer: Medical bias in the health care of gay men*. Binghamton, N.Y.: Harrington Park Press.

———. 1999b. A ride on the wild side. *Poz*, February, 52–55, 70.

———. 1999c. Life after latex. *Poz*, June, 92–93.

Schlossman, S., and R. Cairns. 1993. Problem girls: Observations on past and present. In *Children in time and place: Developmental and historical insights*, ed. G. Elder, J. Modell, and R. Parke. New York: Cambridge University Press.

Schulman, M. 1985. *Bringing up a moral child*. Reading, Mass.: Addison-Wesley.

Sears, J. 1991. *Growing up gay in the South: Race, gender and journeys of the spirit*. New York: Harrington Park Press.

———. 1992. Dilemmas and possibilities of sexuality education: Reproducing the body politic. In *Sexuality and the curriculum: The politics and practices of sexuality education*, ed. J. Sames, 7–33. New York: Teachers College Press.

———. 1995. Black-gay or gay-black: Choosing identities and identifying choices. In *The gay teen: Educational practice and theory for lesbian, gay, and bisexual adolescents*, ed. G. Unks, 135–58. New York: Routledge.

Sedgwick, E. 1993. How to bring your kids up gay. In *Fear of a queer planet*, ed. M. Warner, 69–81. Minneapolis: University of Minnesota Press.

Seelye, K. Q. 1994. Senate cuts money to schools that accept homosexuality. *New York Times*, August 2.

Seidman, S. 1991. *Romantic longings*. New York: Routledge.

———. 1992. *Embattled eros: Sexual politics and ethics in contemporary America*. New York: Routledge.

Sharp, S., and P. Smith, eds. 1994. *Tackling bullying in your school: A practical handbook for teachers*. London: Routledge.

Shoop, R. 1994. *How to stop sexual harassment in our schools: A handbook and curriculum guide for administrators and teachers*. Boston: Allyn and Bacon.

Silin, J. 1995. *Sex, death, and the education of children: Our passion for ignorance in the age of AIDS*. New York: Teachers College Press.

———. 1997. The pervert in the classroom. In *Making a place for pleasure in early childhood education*, ed. J. Tobin, 214–34. New Haven, Conn.: Yale University Press.

Skelton, C. 1994. Sex, male teachers and young children. *Gender and Education* 6 (1): 90.

Skolnick, A. 1976. *Rethinking childhood: Perspectives on development and society*. Boston: Little, Brown.

Smith, P., and Y. Morita. 1999. Introduction. In *The nature of school bullying: A cross-national perspective*, ed. P. K. Smith, Y. Morita, J. Junger-Tas, D. Olweus, R. Catalano, and P. Slee, 1–4. New York: Routledge.

Sommerville, C. J. 1982. *The rise and fall of childhood*. Beverly Hills, Calif.: Sage.

Sonnie, A., ed. 2000. *Revolutionary voices*. Los Angeles: Alyson.

Stacey, J. 1991. *Brave new families*. New York: Basic Books.

Stanford University. 1994–1995a. *Courses, degrees, and information*. Palo Alto, Calif.

Stanford University. 1994–1995b. *School of Education information bulletin*. Palo Alto, Calif.

State University of New York at Buffalo. 1993–1996. *Graduate School of Education*. New York.

Stein, N. 1996. *Bullyproof: A teacher's guide on teasing and bullying*. Wellesley, Mass.: Wellesley College Center for Research on Women.

Stein, N., and D. Cappello. 1999. *Gender violence, gender justice*. Wellesley, Mass.: Wellesley College Center for Research on Women.

Stevenson, R. B., and J. Ellis. 1993. Dropouts and the silencing of critical voices. In *Beyond silenced voices: Class, race, and gender in United States schools*, ed. L. Weis and M. Fine. Albany: State University of New York Press.

Stop AIDS. 2000. *HIV stops with me*. San Francisco: Stop AIDS Project.

Strong, S. 1996. *Rocky Horror schoolgirl*. In *Generation Q*, ed. R. Bernstein and S. Silberman. Los Angeles: Alyson.

Sullivan, A. 1995. *Virtually normal: An argument about homosexuality*. New York: Knopf.

Sullivan, L. W. 1989. Correspondence to congressman William E. Dannemeyer, October 13. Human Rights Campaign Fund, Washington, D.C.

Takanishi, R. 1978. Childhood as a social issue: Historical roots of contemporary child advocacy movements. *Journal of Social Issues* 34 (2): 8–28.

Teachers College. 1994–1995. *Course catalogue.* New York: Columbia University Press.

Teaching teachers. 1995. *Newsweek*, April 2, 69.

Teaching teachers: Graduate schools of education face intense scrutiny. 1995b. *U.S. News and World Report*, April 3, 69–71.

Terrence Higgins Trust and Community HIV and AIDS Prevention Strategy. 2001a. *Facts for life.* London: Terrence Higgins Trust.

———. 2001b. *In two minds?* London: Terrence Higgins Trust.

Terry, J. 1999. *An American obsession: Science, medicine, and the place of homosexuality in modern society.* Chicago: University of Chicago Press.

Third World Gay Revolution. 1972. What we want, what we believe. In *Out of the closets: Voices of gay liberation*, ed. K. Jay and A. Young, 363–67. New York: Douglas.

Thorne, B. 1993. *Gender play: Girls and boys in school.* New Brunswick, N.J.: Rutgers University Press.

Tierney, W. 1992. Building academic communities of difference: Gays, lesbians, and bisexuals on campus. *Change* 24 (2): 44.

Tierney, W., and R. Rhoads. 1993. Enhancing academic communities for lesbian, gay, and bisexual faculty. *New Directions for Teaching and Learning*, 53 (Spring): 43.

Tyack, D. 1974. *The one best system.* Cambridge, Mass.: Harvard University Press.

Unks, G., ed. 1995a. *The gay teen: Educational practice and theory for lesbian, gay, and bisexual adolescents.* New York: Routledge.

Unks, G. 1995b. Thinking about the gay teen. In *The gay teen: Educational practice and theory for lesbian, gay, and bisexual adolescents*, ed. G. Unks, 3–12. New York: Routledge.

University of California at Berkeley. 1994. Social and cultural studies in education—Ph.D. program. In *Graduate School of Education.*

———. 1994–1995. *Graduate School of Education.*

University of Chicago. 1994–1995. *Graduate studies in education.*

University of Massachusetts at Amherst. 1994–1995. *Graduate School bulletin.*

University of North Carolina at Chapel Hill. n.d. *Shaping your future in education.*

University of North Carolina at Chapel Hill. 1993–1994. *School of Education.*

University of Southern California. 1994–1995. Dean's message. In *School of Education bulletin,* 6. Los Angeles.

University of Wisconsin at Madison. 1993–1995. *School of Education bulletin.*

U.S. Department of Health and Human Services. 1989. *Report on the secretary's task force on youth suicide.* Recommendation 6d-2. Washington, D.C.: GPO.

U.S. marriage is weakening, study reports. 1999. *New York Times*, July 4, 12.

U.S. Surgeon General: Suicide rate high among gay teenagers. 1994. *San Francisco Sentinel*, September 28, 22.

Vaid, U. 1995. *Virtual equality: The mainstreaming of lesbian and gay liberation.* New York: Doubleday.

Valentine, J. 1992. *The daddy machine.* Boston: Alyson Wonderland.

———. 1993. *Two moms, the Zark, and me.* Boston: Alyson Wonderland.

Van Bronkhorst, E. 1994. Gay students in Seattle public schools said to face daunting array of abuses. *Bay Windows* (Boston), September 8, 8.

Vandals deface journals at U. of New Mexico. 1994. *Chronicle of Higher Education,* December 7, A4.

Verhellen, E., and E. Spiesschaert, eds. 1994. *Children's rights: Monitoring issues.* Ghent, Belg.: Meys and Breesch.

Von Uhl, K. 1995. Des Moines school board member comes out of the closet. *San Francisco Bay Times,* February 9.

Walkowitz, J. 1992. *City of dreadful delight: Narratives of sexual danger in late-Victorian London,* Chicago: University of Chicago Press.

Walling, D., ed. 1996. *Open lives, safe schools: Addressing gay and lesbian issues in education.* Bloomington, Ind.: Phi Delta Kappa Educational Foundation.

Walsh, P. 1994. The Northeastern news. *U. Magazine,* October, 5.

Walsh, S. 1995a, March 3. Anti-gay forces get personal in fight over sex ed. *Washington Blade,* 6.

———. 1995b. Education department takes "a pretty important step." *Washington Blade,* March 3, 27.

———. 1995c. Fairfax debate nears final hour. *Washington Blade,* March 10, 5.

———. 1995d. Fairfax approves sex ed. plan. *Washington Blade,* March 17, 6.

Warschaw, T. A., and D. Barlow. 1995. *Resiliency: How to bounce back faster, stronger, smarter.* New York: Master Media.

Watney, S. 1991. School's out. In *Inside/out: Lesbian theories, gay theories,* ed. D. Fuss. New York: Routledge.

Ways and means. 1995. *Chronicle of Higher Education,* February 10, A29.

Weeks, J. 1979. *Coming out: Homosexual politics in Britain, from the nineteenth century to the present.* London: Quartet Books.

———. 1991. *Against nature: Essays on history, sexuality, and identity.* London: River Oram Press.

Weiss, M. 1995. Father says he's proud son wore gay shirt to school. *Bay Windows* (Boston), February 23, 15.

Wheelock College. 1994–1995. *Graduate catalogue.* Boston.

Whisman, V. 1995. *Queer by choice: Lesbians, gay men, and the politics of identity.* New York: Routledge.

Willhoite, M. 1991. *Families: A coloring book.* Boston: Alyson Wonderland.

———. 1992. *The entertainer.* Boston: Alyson Wonderland.

Willis, P. 1977. *Learning to labour.* London: Gower.

Wilson, R. 1995. Lecture on female masturbation harassed him, male student says. *Chronicle of Higher Education,* March 17, A18.

Wittman, C. 1972. A gay manifesto. In *Out of the closets: Voices of gay liberation,* ed. K. Jay and A. Young. New York: Douglas.

Woodhead, M. 1990. Psychology and the cultural construction of children's needs. In *Constructing and reconstructing childhood: Contemporary issues in the sociological study of childhood,* ed. A. James and A. Prout. New York: Falmer.

Woog, D. 1995. *School's out: The impact of gay and lesbian issues on America's schools.* Boston: Alyson Publications.

World Health Organization. 1996. *The Ottawa charter for health promotion.* Geneva: Author. i

Yang, A. 1997. *From wrongs to rights: Public opinion on gay and lesbian Americans moves toward equality.* Washington, D.C.: National Gay and Lesbian Task Force Policy Institute.

Yeskel, F. 1985. The consequence of being gay: A report on the quality of life for lesbian, gay, and bisexual students at the University of Massachusetts at Amherst. Office of the Vice Chancellor for Student Affairs, Amherst, Mass.

Youth Liberation of Ann Arbor. 1972. *Youth liberation.* Washington, N.J.: Times Change Press.

Index